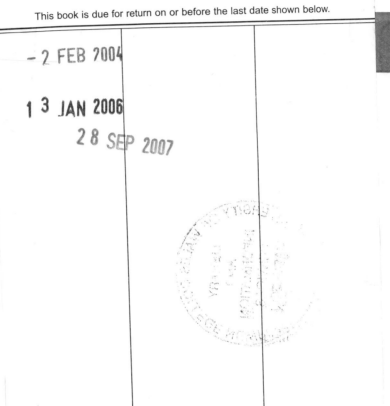
By Chris Wardle and Tina Rae

Illustrated by Tina Rae

These materials were developed in close collaboration with Bristol Schools.

Published by Lucky Duck Publishing Ltd
3 Thorndale Mews, Clifton, Bristol
BS8 2HX, UK

Commissioned by George Robinson
Edited by Sara Perraton
Book Design by Barbara Maines
Cover Design by Hellen weller
Printed in the UK by The Book Factory, Mildway Avenue, London N1 4RS

Dedication

To all the adults and young people that we have worked with over the years, who have contributed to the development of our thinking and ideas and without whom we wouldn't have survived.

Contents

- Key concepts
- Illustrative script
- Teaching the concept
- P.S.

- Beliefs
- Exploring what I believe
- The key belief behind school survival
- The key to the future – saving lives

- Key questions
- Developing and looking for resources
- Key inputs – what should be covered in an intervention?
- Some practical pointers
- The flexible group
- Communicating with others

Introduction and Background

This book aims to support teachers in increasing their own understanding of the difficulties that some students experience in coping with school – particularly in the area of behaviour. It aims to promote a different way of looking at behaviour change in school, and to give practical strategies and ways of approaching difficult students which will hopefully further ensure their inclusion in the mainstream context.

In the past few years and in the foreseeable future the Government has targeted truancy and school exclusion in an attempt to dramatically reduce both and thereby increase social inclusion. Therefore, it will be vital for schools and LEAs to reflect upon their current systems and to ensure that the best possible systems are in place to successfully address student's disaffection and disruptive behaviour. The future focus will consequently need to be in early intervention and support at the earliest stage. Unfortunately, for many schools, the gap between rhetoric and practice still results in a system of crisis management, i.e. support is provided at the stage when student's behaviour has become fully entrenched and relationships are on the verge of collapse. Schools clearly need to address this fact as a matter of priority and must begin to ensure that they adopt preventative approaches to working with groups of students who are at risk of exclusion. It is hopeful that *School Survival* will be able to provide teachers with such an approach.

The book does not aim to provide a definitive structure or content for such an intervention, but rather encourages teachers to develop their own skills and strategies in dealing with difficult students who are perceived to be at risk of exclusion now, or in the future. Clearly, it would be preferable if schools could have identified pupils at an earlier, rather than later, stage in the process. *School Survival* encourages teachers to set up and construct a course that will effectively meet the individual needs of each member of the target group, and ensure that they can and do develop the skills in order to both survive and succeed in school. There is a clear emphasis on utilising the power that is intrinsic to group work and the importance of measuring successful outcomes, i.e. the extent to which 'group skills' are transferred to the classroom context. Whilst the book does not present a structured course for teachers to deliver in sequence, it does provide a wealth of ideas, strategies and tools for the teacher to use in constructing and delivering a successful intervention.

How to Use This Book

The introductory pages will explore some of the key philosophies that underlie the *School Survival* intervention ideas. They will then look at some of the areas that would need to be covered before an intervention was set up and started.

The ideas, strategies and tools which are the basis for this type of intervention, are presented within 10 key concept chapters:

Key concepts

1. Looking for the Best Possible Outcome
2. Looking at Behaviour – Teaching the Students to Analyse and Reflect
3. Using Targets
4. Being Cool in School
5. It's Not Fair
6. Power to the Pupil
7. Don't Tell Me, Show Me
8. It's for Real – Getting the Talk Into the Classroom
9. Using the School Discipline Structure as a Framework
10. Working With a Model

Each section of the book introduces and defines each of these concepts and then proceeds to explain to the teacher how these can be presented to the students and incorporated into the programme as a whole. It is important to realise that although the concepts are presented in an order, this is by no means an order of importance or indeed the order they would need to be covered in an intervention or course that may emerge from this book. It would be important to have an overview and an understanding of how each of the key concepts fits in with the others. This is particularly important in relation to those concepts that promote a certain use of language (i.e. looking at behaviour) or encourage motivators for behavioural change (i.e. using targets and power to the pupil).

Illustrative script

In order to further clarify the concept, an illustrative script is used and provides a 'real life' example of how this can be taught to the students and used by them in order to effect a change in behaviour. A range of teaching methods, ideas and resources are then provided so that the teacher can choose the input or ideas that he/she feels will best meet the needs of their target students.

Teaching the concept

These sections give guidance on possible strategies to teach and help the student understand the specific concepts.

In order to further develop understanding and give practical examples of teaching methods and possible responses, 'Making it Real' diagrams and illustrations are set within the text.

P.S.

These 'Postscript' sections are set at the end of each key concept and offer further practical advice and ideas regarding the teaching and development of these ideas with the students.

Hold on There, Before You Start...

Beliefs

School Survival does not intend to negate any systemic approach. What is a new slant here is the child-focused element that runs throughout each of the key concepts. This is vital if we are to really effect a change in behaviour and allow students to develop their own survival skills. Accepting that our beliefs and perceptions are what drive and produce our behaviours is consequently a major focus – both for students and for the adults involved in supporting them. What also needs to be highlighted here, is the extent to which our beliefs and perceptions will also be what drive the intervention. Some beliefs and perceptions will gain a better outcome than others and it is vital that any teacher attempting to change pupil behaviour and create/ construct an intervention should be aware of their own beliefs and perceptions and the ways in which these may or may not effect the best outcome. It is vital to ensure that you know what you believe, why you believe it, and the kind of behaviours and outcomes that result from your personal belief system.

What is not being presented here is any notion of 'right' or 'wrong' beliefs. What is being presented is the fact that certain beliefs will ensure a better outcome for an individual student in a certain context whilst others will ensure that the student will simply fail. What the facilitator/ teacher needs to continually ask is 'Are my beliefs preventing that student from achieving the best possible outcome, and if so, how do I need to change them to enable the student to succeed?'

Exploring what I believe

We have found it useful to prompt those teachers undertaking this kind of intervention to reflect upon their beliefs with reference to a 'key belief' questionnaire. It is the intention here to stimulate and encourage facilitators and anyone working with young people, to question and reflect upon their own beliefs, identifying where those beliefs may have an impact upon their practice. Each statement within the questionnaire demands the facilitator to identify if they agree or disagree and then to reflect upon the following:

- Why do I agree or disagree?
- What is my own experience that supports or does not support the statement?
- How does holding this belief affect my practice?
- Is my belief shared amongst my colleagues?
- How does holding or not holding these beliefs affect the students that I work with?

Obviously there are no right or wrong answers here, simply a set of circumstances which may or may not lead to the best possible outcomes for the students.

You may wish to consider these statements at this stage in the School Survival programme:

1. Teachers need to change the way they teach to accommodate children with behaviour problems.

    true or false

2. Children are more likely to behave badly when the teaching is poor.

    true or false

3. All pupils have control over their behaviour.

    true or false

4. Badly behaved pupils should be excluded from mainstream school and sent to special school.

    true or false

5. All children are best educated in mainstream school.

    true or false

6. It is not the classteacher's responsibility to deal with behaviour.

    true or false

7. Badly behaved pupils are the responsibility of the pastoral heads and the leadership team.

    true or false

8. I came into teaching to teach my subject not to
    teach behaviour.

    true or false

9. The children have changed in the past few years. I
    should change my teaching to meet those changes.

    true or false

10. Children are born poorly behaved.

    true or false

11. Too much time and money is spent on the
    badly behaved.

    true or false

12. Discipline in schools has got worse in the past
    few years.

    true or false

13. Teachers can't make a difference to the way these pupils
    behave when you look at their home backgrounds.

    true or false

14. Class groupings should be based on behaviour
    and effort.

    true or false

15. Behaviour can be controlled by concentrating on
    the quality of teaching.

    true or false

It is important that teachers and those working with young people are continually challenged about the kinds of beliefs and views they hold with regards to behaviour. Central to our work in *School Survival* is the view of the student – 'If I believe they think I'm bad – I'll be bad'. If the reader does not share this key belief, then we would suggest that making use of this approach in order to design an intervention to ensure student's inclusion is very much redundant. If the teacher holds the view that badly behaved pupils should be withdrawn from the mainstream, then any intervention will need to be provided out of the school context, i.e. in a unit. The beliefs will drive the intervention and consequently need to be identified prior to starting such a course. If the approach presented in *School Survival* is to be adopted, then the facilitator or teacher will need to share a range of key beliefs with the authors. For example:

- Pupils can change their behaviours and be responsible for them
- All individuals have the capacity to change
- All individuals have the capacity to learn
- All behaviour has meaning – there is a reason for students behaving 'like that', and it is not because they are intrinsically 'evil'
- Pupils need to be able to maintain their position within the 'peer hierarchy' and have a right to have their self-esteem and confidence protected and built upon by learning alongside and with their peers in the classroom
- Pupils should be taught the skills and strategies that they will need in order to survive and succeed in school, i.e. develop and maintain their own Survival Kit bags and pull out what they need when they need it
- Pupils and adults have the right to air their own beliefs and to have these heard and respected
- Those who design and deliver these interventions always need to understand, appreciate and attempt to affect positive changes in the beliefs of those who are teaching the students on a daily basis

It is vital for the facilitator to be very much aware of his or her own set of key beliefs and values. It is these beliefs that will drive the intervention and very much feed into the course content, direction and the approaches adopted. What is essential is that these beliefs are those that will ensure that the student within the group can and does move forward, and finds themselves in a better position having achieved the best possible outcome for themselves. The facilitator will need to continually engage in the reflective cycle in order to plan the intervention, evaluate outcomes and then change both beliefs and practices in order to once again aim for the best possible outcome.

These key beliefs and the way in which they may be reformulated and altered on a continual basis are linked to the context in which the facilitator or teacher is working. It is vital that we understand and fully appreciate what the system is in each situation. Such a systemic approach would also allow for a genuine acknowledgement of teacher stress and patterns of behaviour – what we have to contend and cope with on a daily basis. There is no emphasis here on apportioning blame - this is purely a process of clarifying exactly what the situation is and what it is that we can change in order to make the context less stressful and more productive for all involved. It is within such a context that the *School Survival* intervention can be implemented. We need to work with the existing pressures and contexts and acknowledge those pressures that we can change and those that we can't.

This process of acknowledgement can be further clarified by means of the mirror diagram below. This illustration attempts to provide an understanding of the systems within which both the teacher and the student are currently working. The stressors or non-changeable pressures and the changeable pressures for both parties appear to be remarkably similar, even when the pressure from continual government initiatives and inspection, which teachers will have to cope with, are reflected within the student's curriculum. Both the teachers and students need to understand how their personal pressures are, to some extent, interchangeable, and how both acknowledging and attempting to cope with and change some of these is generally a two way process.

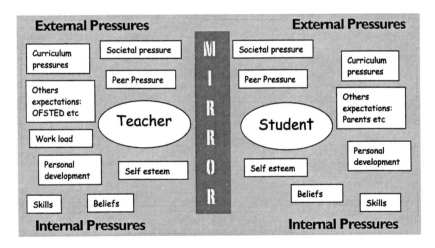

What is necessary is for both teachers and students to develop all the skills and strategies that they will need in order to cope with these pressures and survive in a range of social contexts, but especially at school! It is hoped that the concepts covered in *School Survival* will enable positive outcomes and knock-on effects for the teachers and others involved.

The key belief behind school survival

As previously stated, *School Survival* promotes and presents the key belief that any intervention needs to be child-focused. The key is about empowering the individual students to be able to develop in such a way as to survive all that school demands of them. The intervention is set up to encourage change at the level of the student.

Unfortunately, in our experience, the more that teachers in classrooms struggle with behaviour, the more they tend to blame the children and adopt a negative and often punitive stance. The problem in this stressed and emotive environment is laid squarely upon the individual students. Consequently, when attempting to support such teachers, it is very often necessary to pull them back from being 'child-focused' in this way, in order to consider further what it is that they themselves can do in terms of developing their own classroom management strategies and techniques. The idea here is that the right change in the system or context should allow for the inclusion of all students.

The move in the development of teacher's skills is away from the child-focused approach. However, it is this very child-focused approach which is what *School Survival* unashamedly adopts and reinforces, i.e. you have got this problem and you can change it – we can help you, but it's you who has to change it!

Ironically, this message can be of use in allaying the fears of those teachers who wish to blame the students rather than attempt to change their own methods or style of teaching:
"That's fine if you want them to change their behaviour, as it confirms my beliefs that it's not me who's at fault – I don't need to change, but they do!"

However, it is, of course, still essential that such teachers do in fact manage their classrooms as well as they possibly can in order to really give the students the best chance of surviving. What may appear to be the most trivial change to a school's expectations or routine may, in fact, be the crucial aspect that really does save the student's life in that school context. Dramatic but true. *School Survival* – the child-focused approach, is very definitely not a replacement for good classroom management. It is an attempt to meet the needs of individuals and to help them survive in school. It is not a 'trivial' subject.

This approach takes the view that however students may present themselves on the surface as being disaffected and not wanting to co-operate and be in school, this is not what really motivates them or what they really believe. In our experience of working with such groups, all students really want is to be 'in school' and to be coping effectively within that context. There are very, very few students we have met who actually do not want to be in school.

The key to the future – saving lives

School Survival aims to teach the students the skills and strategies they need in order to stay in school - both now and in the future. Getting excluded is not an option, but keeping on the right track and being helped to do so by those around you certainly is. A permanent exclusion can change and damage a student's life forever. The whole purpose of constructing and delivering this kind of intervention is to ensure that these lives are saved and not lost in this way. It is vital that both students and adults in the school context are not blind as to the consequences for those students who are permanently excluded from school, and part of this intervention needs to ensure accurate definition of the facts surrounding this process. Being kept in school is what can and does change the course of the individual's life for the better. It is the key to future successes and we, as adults, have the responsibility to see that the students have the skills to pick up and use the key, and thus be able to open the door to a successful future life.

Getting Ready To Go!

Key questions

The principles discussed earlier clearly set out quite a challenge as regards the planning and implementation of a useful intervention. We would stress that this can be made easier if the initial planning process has been thorough and systematic. Below are a range of questions, which when answered before constructing the course, will help the process of planning as well as encourage the facilitator to reflect on just what it is they are trying to do.

- What are the aims of intervention?
- What is the intervention model that we are going to use to help meet these aims?
- Which pupils is this for?
- What do we hope to achieve?
- What is the structure of the course?
- What is the structure of the week?
- What is the structure of a lesson? What curriculum are we following?
- Who will staff this intervention?
- How do we set the expectations for the course and for behaviour when on the course?
- What contact should we have with parents?
- What type of needs can the course meet?
- How does the unit fit in with the rest of the school?
- How is good communication maintained?
- How and when do we set targets?
- How do we and the students know when we have been successful?
- How can the students be rewarded?
- How do we monitor the students and how do they monitor themselves?
- What happens at the end of the course?
- How do we support the students in the classroom?

- What support is going to be offered at the end of the course?
- How can we increase the transference from group into class?

Clearly, if the facilitator is able to address each of these questions (not necessarily in this order), then the job of constructing, delivering, maintaining and measuring the success of the intervention should be much more straightforward.

Developing and looking for resources

Given that this publication aims to further promote an understanding of how group interventions can help students survive and succeed at school, it will necessarily follow that any group facilitator will also develop an understanding and awareness as to what should be included in the course. We aim to be reasonably explicit about what might be included and covered in an intervention. However, we are very aware that those who use this resource will also see the need to develop their own range of skills and resources alongside further investigating and making use of a wide range of published resources as well – some of which we will refer to along the way.

Key inputs – what should be covered in an intervention?

Tell it as it is – give the best information to aid the best understanding.

For many facilitators, the content of the intervention occupies a great deal of the initial concern and planning time.

Throughout this book we hope to offer guidance. However, it is important that, whatever the intervention, every concept, idea, strategy and technique will be fully explained and presented to the students in the best possible way, giving them the best possible understanding of what they are trying to do. Often, when working with young people, the understanding and reasons behind behavioural change in the form of theory and strategies are withheld, albeit with the good intention of not complicating the issues with complex and 'adult' models. However, it is our belief that young people are often more than capable of understanding these 'complex' theories and models, often because they ring true in their understanding of the situation, and that discussing underlying psychological models or physiological process can only aid understanding and the subsequent behavioural change. The facilitator may have to adjust or simplify some of the language used, but the concepts taught will remain the same as those that would be presented to those adults who may be trying to understand student behaviour.

This means that the students are provided with the fullest and most detailed explanation possible - whether this is about the physiology, the locus of control, the psychology of behaviour etc.

Understanding the psychology of behaviour - how and why we behave in the way that we do and how we can change and gain control over our behaviours - is central to this course. It is essential that the students are provided with such a basis, knowledge and understanding if they are to move forward and gain more positive outcomes for themselves. As adults, we can work within the social systems and contexts and survive because we do, on the whole, have this kind of knowledge. If we provide the same knowledge for the students, then it is clearly more likely that they can and will survive the school system. The knowledge and information simply has to be provided in their context.

It is evident that the framework of the *School Survival* course is indeed 'a framework'. It also adopts and presents, from the outset, a young person-focused approach. Consequently, although we suggest a series of concepts and provide a range of strategies, techniques and ideas within these, we do not dictate the actual content of the course session by session. There are, of course, included within our suggestions, many things that probably should be included and taught, i.e. a 'core' set of ideas. We strongly believe that it is the make-up of the group itself and the particular needs and aspirations of each student that should actually dictate the context of the course. What is eventually included should be very much a direct result of the group working together and the group dynamics. This is, of course, far more complicated and time-consuming than simply strictly adhering to any one particular set programme. Obviously, the students may gain from an 'off the peg' intervention, but we are convinced that really placing the work within their context, environment and culture, and allowing them to have more than a superficial voice and input, will produce more positive results and effect 'owned' behaviours and change.

The structure and content of the course also need to be flexible in order to address and attempt to meet the specific targets of each individual student within the group. They will all have different targets and will consequently all demand different inputs in order to gain the skills and knowledge needed to meet the targets. However, notwithstanding this fact, it is generally a good idea to provide the group of students with a course structure, i.e. an idea of what each session may cover - even if it's not necessarily that order that is kept to. They need to be able to visualise their way through the course. They need to be able to see the 'big picture' and to be able to say 'It's Monday, and so we're doing this'.

It is also important to immediately gain the student's interest in the context of each of the sessions by presenting the topic in an entertaining and immediate way. For example, snappy titles/ subject headings such as 'My Excellent Future' and 'My Body as a Spaceship' can be used to introduce strategies of future planning, motivation and basic physiology. Having the content made more specific in this way also reinforces the fact that these sessions are 'lessons' and that the students will be expected to learn from them.

Whilst it is important that any intervention should be tailor-made in order to meet the requirements of those students involved, we would recommend that facilitators make reference to the following list of key inputs. These can be used as a basic framework on which to plan and design the course. We have certainly tended to make reference to this list in our own planning procedures:

- Surviving school – how can I do this? How do others succeed?
- Looking at my behaviour – learning the descriptive language
- Looking at other's behaviour – developing observational skills
- Anger management – developing my own skills
- How I think – the way my brain works
- Using targets to plan and to effect changes in my behaviour
- Conflict resolution – learning the skills
- Simple physiology – knowing why I do what I do
- Locus of control – learning to have internal control
- What is it like to be a teacher? – developing empathy and understanding
- Looking into the future – what happens next?
- My excellent future – getting motivated
- Group building – supporting each other in the group
- Secret signs – supporting each other out of the group
- Body language – learning to read it
- Saying sorry like I mean it
- How to have a good argument
- How to get what I want without getting into trouble

Some practical pointers

In the same way as we have said before, the facilitator will need to consider the practical issues of their intervention in terms of the system in which they are working. However, this list (which is by no means exhaustive) may give some guidance in the initial stages of setting up an intervention:

Where should I hold the sessions?

Some facilitators may have the luxury of a base or a classroom that can provide a consistent and safe place. However, do not be put off if this is not the case. Some of the best and most powerful interventions are held in the classrooms where the students have their difficulties in the first place. As long as the place where the sessions may take place is planned in advance, the sessions can take place anywhere. Indeed, there may be some advantages in holding the sessions in a variety of different settings, as this may increase the likelihood of the skills being transferable.

How long should the sessions be?

Generally, we would hold the sessions in the same length of time that the lessons exist within. It is easier to timetable and has the advantage of 'training' the students to become used to the time slot, over which, they will need to survive.

What size of group?

This will depend greatly on what you are trying to achieve, but in general no bigger than eight and no smaller than four for the initial intervention. Bigger groups give more practice at developing the survival skills surrounded by more individuals (like in a classroom), and smaller groups mean that the intervention can be more precisely targeted.

How often should we meet?

At least once a week and possibly twice. In the initial stages of the intervention it is important to meet more often to set the momentum of the group.

How long should the intervention run?

Again, this will depend greatly on what you are trying to achieve, but probably no less than six weeks and no longer (for one individual group) than 12 weeks.

The flexible group

A central aim of the *School Survival* intervention is that of maximising the use of group process. The facilitator's role will clearly be that of listening, reflecting and eliciting the ideas and views of the students, and the group structure should enable these students to participate in these processes and empower them to effect change. The non directive approach detailed in this book reinforces the principle that the group should be flexible at all times. Such an approach does maximise the group process and is extremely powerful in terms of inspiring and effecting change. Some facilitators / teachers may, initially, find this approach slightly daunting if they have previously adopted a more directive approach in planning and implementing such interventions.

Directive approaches may initially feel 'safer' in that they are clearly time constrained and the activities / curriculum to be covered is set out in a clear step by step manner, which is easy to follow and deliver. Naturally, as with non-directive approaches, group processes and skills development will be ongoing, including the building of relationships, discussions about feelings, provision of a sense of belonging, development of social skills, and the development of working practices etc. However, we would suggest that where there is a balance between the two approaches, as is the line in *School Survival*, then the students have the greatest possibility of success and the work done is far more powerful. The balance between the directive approach, i.e. course curriculum, and the non-directive approach which allows for what the students bring to the group and is led more by where the students are, is the flexible approach that we would recommend in order to achieve the best possible outcome.

Throughout each of the 10 key concepts sections, there is a continual emphasis upon flexibility and on the teacher to both provide a structure and ensure that there is room for manoeuvre within this structure at all times. This will mean allowing the students to contribute to the course contents by clarifying their own needs and requirements. The facilitator will be knowledgeable, secure and skilled in order to achieve such flexibility and to allow for the best possible outcome to be achieved by each student. Analysing and reflecting further upon the course content is central to the role of the facilitator throughout the whole period of this intervention.

Communicating with others

Communicating with teachers

The philosophy that underpins this intervention is very much rooted in humanistic principles with the focus on the possibility and necessity of the students being able to change themselves and their behaviours for the better – even in the face of adversity! Students will need to be aware of the contextual drives to their behaviour, but at the same time the course asks them to focus more fundamentally upon themselves. Central to this intervention is the notion of the student having control of his own destiny and not being, or feeling, controlled by others.

However, it is obvious that the student will have a greater chance of achieving this success and control, and obtaining the best possible outcome, if a number of key people are 'on side' and genuinely supporting the intervention. This support can be offered either directly to the student or can be given via the whole school culture and ethos. It is important to understand the extent to which working with smaller groups of students within a whole school context can be quite isolating. There is clearly a danger of the facilitator being perceived as the one who 'works with' and 'sticks up for' those 'naughty kids'. Emotionally, this can be quite draining on the facilitator. He will frequently be involved in ensuring or attempting to ensure that those involved with the student do make a positive contribution to the change process; whilst also attempting to set up and develop a culture in the school which is supportive, both to the facilitator and to the students themselves.

It is clearly vital that the teachers in the school actually understand what is going on in terms of the *School Survival* intervention. The facilitator needs to ensure that teacher/facilitator liaison is ongoing and constructive at all times. The facilitator will need to gain the support of staff and encourage a continual positive dialogue in order to find out exactly what is going on in the classroom. He will need this information in order to know what needs to change and to plan the appropriate programme of support for the student. The facilitator will need to be continually aware of the extent to which the teacher's views, perceptions and descriptions of student's behaviour will be tainted with emotion. The students will often have been the cause of the teacher's stress and may have been continually 'winding them up' long before the facilitator entered the scenario. The dialogue and information can, therefore, be tainted with a great deal of associated negative emotions and it may not be particularly useful. The aim is therefore to obtain truly objective information about behaviour, about what the teacher is doing, and what is and isn't successful. The teacher's objective descriptions need to be sensibly drawn out by the facilitator to then enable the student and facilitator to specifically target and work upon these difficulties or 'problem' areas.

A further reason for developing and maintaining positive lines of communication, and for ensuring that teachers really know what the intervention is about, is that it enables the intervention to be set within the context of the school's discipline policy and procedures. Unfortunately, in our experience, these policies are generally not implemented consistently throughout the school. It is therefore important that the teachers are made aware of how the facilitator will be closely monitoring the consistency of delivery of these policies in order to attempt to ensure that the students really do have the best chance of achieving the best possible outcome for themselves. Also, it is crucial that the teachers are aware of the fact that there will be consequences for the students if they are unable to meet the requirements of the school's disciplinary procedures. If, for example, the student's target is not to be thrown out of class on more than two occasions in any given week, then in order to achieve this, he will not only need to try as hard as possible, but the teachers will also need to be absolutely consistent in the way in which they monitor and implement the behaviour management system. It would be a problem if one member of staff decided to bypass the 'usual' procedures and simply eject the pupil for the most minor of incidents. Clearly, this is a case of 'it's not fair' for the student and, as discussed earlier, there may be a mediation role for the facilitator to take here.

The fact that, prior to this intervention, the relationship between the students and some or many of the teachers in the school will have broken down, is something that will continually need to be addressed in order to overcome the barriers to those students actually going back into the classroom. Again, the teacher/facilitator dialogue is essential if the student is to be successful. Without the dialogue, the student could well be making the greatest of efforts to change, but because their efforts do not include, or appear to include, the relationship that they have with the teacher, then the teacher may well not recognise these efforts and subsequently may not make an effort themselves to change their responses to the student or to compromise or meet them halfway. If the facilitator makes the teacher aware of the process of change and the personal reflection and effort experienced by the student, i.e. ensures continual feedback and constructive liaison, then this kind of problem can be avoided or minimised to some extent. If the teacher is made aware of the actual processes undergone by the student, this should inform and hopefully impact positively on their own responses to that student.

Without continual constructive dialogue and liaison, some teachers may well adopt the stance of 'what is going on in that group?' or 'why haven't they been cured?'. This is clearly a worst case scenario and of course it can generally be avoided if the facilitator works effectively to keep the teachers informed so that they have realistic expectations of the students and accurate knowledge about the movement or changes that students may have made. The principles underpinning the intervention and the key themes and ideas need to be explained and outlined to staff (possibly both verbally and in writing), both at the outset of the intervention and at regular intervals along the way. It will be particularly important to ensure, for example, that teachers fully appreciate and understand the notion or concept of moving to a 'better' position. The facilitator's line may consequently need to be: 'Yes, I know it's not entirely satisfactory at the moment – but can you see any movement in the right direction?' The response, even if grudging, may be 'yes, I suppose so', which is, of course, another step entirely in the right direction!

Communicating with the teachers also helps to ensure that the students can receive the best, most informed and precise support. When the facilitator is working with a group of students in this way, the knowledge that they gain of each student is clearly invaluable in terms of aiding the process of change. It is possible to identify the things that individual teachers might be able to change in terms of their own practice in order to help and support these students. However, it is important to clarify that this is rather different from providing teachers with advice on behaviour management (although we recognise that all teachers will need such advice and training at different points in their working lives). This type of consultation and feedback is, in effect, a system of 'fine tuning' responses and behaviours – a 'minimal' activity which will hopefully ensure the maximum effect in terms of moving the students on - even if this maximum effect, at the time, is a further few minutes inclusion in the classroom context. For example, a 'fine tuning' comment may suggest to a teacher that it has been noted that pupil A generally finds it easier to settle down to the task if the teacher simply puts the work onto his table and then walks away, i.e. expecting Billy to get on and do it and affording him a certain level of responsibility and respect, whilst still showing who's boss and what the expectations are! This case is then about supporting the pupil and the teacher, with the facilitator acting as the intermediary between the two. Clearly, however, it is also about the facilitator being entirely professional and honourable, and not engaging in any form of collusion with either party. The whole focus needs to be on the facilitator passing on their knowledge and understanding of the students to the teachers, to ensure that their knowledge and understanding increases, alongside their repertoire of strategies and skills, in order to successfully support and include the students in their classrooms. The relationship needs to be empowering rather than judgemental – in both directions.

What is essential, of course, is that the teacher is actually willing to be part of such a process. There needs to be an acknowledgement of the fact, not only that the child may be changing, but also that the process may be even more successful if the teacher is also willing and able to make some specific changes and engage in some 'fine tuning' as well. In no sense are we proposing this is an easy option. Most change requires a journey through the pain barrier, and where there is a great deal of history and emotion attached, this process can be difficult for all involved. To a certain extent the process could be said to be representative of the 'no pain, no gain' philosophy! However, it may well be that the ongoing dialogue and work of this kind needs to purely focus upon these one or two teachers who may, in fact, tip the balance in the positive direction for that particular student.

Communicating with pupils

How other pupils perceive the group is clearly important, and aiming to harness their good will and empathy in order to support the targeted students is an enormous, but not insurmountable, task. However, what may initially need to be addressed are the teacher's perceptions of other student's views of the group – particularly if these are negative and in danger of creating or perpetuating resentment towards the group. For example, the unconvinced and possibly angry teacher who has not, as yet, understood the purpose and nature of the intervention may well support the view that these students are receiving some kind of reward for their 'bad' behaviour. Going off to a nice cosy room for little chats, cups of coffee and special treats. Clearly, this is not an accurate perception in any sense, and this jaundiced view needs to be tackled head on.

The facilitator can do this by presenting the intervention to both staff and students in the school as an additional, compulsory subject that this specific group of students needs to incorporate into their timetables. *School Survival* is not a treat in any sense of the word. The students involved will have to work harder than those who do not take this subject, as the processes involved are demanding in terms of the energy, application and commitment involved. The facilitator will need to 'sell' this intervention to the students in such a way that they certainly don't perceive it as a cosy, soft option. Also, it is important to point out that if staff and those students who are 'never in trouble' don't feel that the reward system itself is 'fair' i.e. that 'good' students receive appropriate rewards, then this does need to be addressed. Of course, such students should be acknowledged, recognised, praised and rewarded on a daily basis. If this is not happening, then the systems and policies are simply not right and they will need to be modified to ensure that all students are included in the process. If setting up the *School Survival* intervention results in a revaluation and subsequent reformulation of the school system, then this can only be a positive outcome for all involved – including any students and staff who may have perceived the intervention as being an unfair reward for the badly behaved minority!

What is also vital is that school staff and the facilitator to show that they are taking on board the views of those students who are not involved in the group. They need to be made aware of the fact that the reason they don't have to take the *School Survival* course is that they already have the skills that will be covered in the group sessions. They can cope with and survive the school systems and context without difficulty. The students who will participate in the course are those who can't survive school – they simply don't have those skills. It's not simply about misbehaviour – it's about learning and practising the kinds of skills that will enable them to take control and make the changes that they need to in order to survive and remain included in this context. The facilitator can get this message across to students in a year group assembly or form/tutor time as appropriate. Details of the course, what it's about, and what it involves, all need to be presented in a direct, open and honest way – telling it as it is.

Communicating with parents
This can be both a powerful and an extremely difficult task. Underlying every intervention of this kind is the vital importance of ensuring that the student's parents are 'on side'. They need to be involved in the process of supporting their child's developing skills and they need to be provided with accurate information about the course and given ongoing feedback as appropriate. There is clearly more chance of the student succeeding if the parents are involved and supportive - even to the smallest extent.

During an initial discussion with each parent, we have found it most productive to be totally upfront – again, telling it as it is. For the majority of parents, hearing about their child's negative behaviour patterns and predicaments in school will cause no major surprise or shock. They will probably already have experienced short- or fixed-term exclusions and been made fully aware as to why these were given. However, there may be some parents who are not fully aware of exactly how serious the situation really is, and what the implications are – both for them and their child – if their child is permanently excluded.

The discussion will usually begin with a realistic description of the student's behaviour and this will invariably create a negative picture for the parent. What is important is to ensure that they are not given the message that it's their fault and that they are to blame for this situation. The description needs to be presented in a matter of fact manner avoiding use of any emotive language. The facilitator then needs to explain exactly what the consequences would be of a permanent exclusion. However, this then allows for the more positive scenario and a preferred future to be presented, i.e. we don't want this to happen which is why we're running this course and why we want your child to participate in it. The parents need to get the message that the facilitator, along with school-based staff, does actually want their child to succeed and to stay in school. The evidence of this lies in the fact that they are prepared to devote time, effort and additional resources to try and ensure a better outcome for the student. This is a powerful message and is very often one that the parents weren't expecting to receive, but which they certainly needed to hear. For some parents this may have been the best piece of news they've had for sometime - we have certainly come across many examples of this mixture of relief and surprise during such conversations. They know they're not being sold false dreams, but they are aware that their child is being given a real chance to change and to survive in school. The situation is not without hope and the parents can be provided with a realistic and more optimistic picture than the one presented at the start of the conversation. If their child can make the changes and learn the necessary skills, then the fear of permanent exclusion will disappear.

This points to the need to adopt motivational interview techniques, i.e. encouraging the parent to visualise and talk about what kind of future they want for their child and how they are going to achieve their aims. Such a line of questioning and the adoption of an entirely honest and positive stance should help to prevent the parent from simply becoming angry with their child. This is something that really needs to be avoided entirely. When painting the initially negative picture, the facilitator needs to be careful not to give the parent any opportunity to condemn their child, e.g. "Well, frankly, he's just a little shit and he's like that at home as well". It's not helpful or constructive and certainly won't inspire any hope for the future. The facilitator will continually need to reframe any negatives and ensure that the conversation maintains, and concludes with, a positive outlook.

Clearly there are no set rules as to where and when the initial conversations will take place and arrangements may well be dependant upon the resources available. The minimum consultation we'd envisage would be a telephone, call but what perhaps provides the most powerful message to parents is to have the initial meeting in the home. We would always encourage the student to be present at this meeting in order to create a real climate of openness, honesty and respect for all involved. They need to receive the message that nothing is or will be hidden. This arrangement would also allow for an initial focus on targets and success criteria, and this is important because the parent needs to know when it's going to start to look as if the intervention is being successful. Both parents and students need to be made aware of the fact that there is no magic wand on offer here and that the processes involved may be very difficult to go through. What is important is that they all understand and perceive this intervention as a real movement in the right direction. Parents will need to be encouraged to articulate how they will know when there is a movement in the right direction – what will they see?

Once parents have agreed to their child participating in the *School Survival* course, the facilitator should outline the course content and ensure that they are made aware of what their child will be doing in these sessions – anger management etc. The facilitator can then ask the parents how they would like to be informed of their child's progress. What's the best and most convenient way of doing this for them? Once these arrangements have been agreed, it is vital to set the date for the next meeting and the facilitator can then confirm this in writing. A concise note detailing the agreement made and painting a positive picture of the course can be a helpful way of formalising these arrangements. It is also advisable to make a telephone call or write a short note to parents approximately two weeks into the course in order to let them know that their child is doing well – even if this is putting something of a gloss on events. It is the knock-on effects of creating a positive start that is important here. The parents need to feel positive so that they can also begin to reframe their own relationship with the school and experience positive feedback which, in turn, should have a knock-on effect upon their relationship with their child and, ultimately, their child's behaviour in school. If parents feel okay about their child, then the child will also feel okay about being who they are.

A date for an end of course review/evaluation meeting will also need to be set and kept. Alongside this commitment to regular contact and feedback (whether by telephone, note or meeting), the facilitator may also consider the possibility of setting up a parent's support group. Clearly, this can only be done if the parents wish to participate in this way and if the resources are available – for example, a facilitator, rooms etc. Such groups can provide a non-threatening and supportive network for parents to consider their own relationship with the school, and the messages that they may give to their child about school as an institution. Where a skilled facilitator and the other essential resources are available, such groups have been of enormous benefit to both parents and their children. However, this is the best case scenario, and we are well aware that these kinds of resources may not be available to some schools.

It is also immensely worthwhile considering the role of the student's grandparents in terms of supporting the *School Survival* intervention. In our experience, students often have a grandparent who are very much involved in their lives and concerned about their well-being and future success. In such cases, we have sometimes been able to enlist the support of the grandparent and they have become the one who communicates with us on a regular basis. Because grandparents are, in relationship terms, one step removed from the students, the relationship is often built upon positive indulgence - they want to, and frequently do, see the 'best' in their grandchild and want the best possible outcomes for them. Feeding back positives to an already positive and committed supporter clearly has additional knock on benefits all round.

Illustrative Script
Talking to Mum

Mum: I suppose you're going to tell me what a pain in the arse Michael is and I won't be arguing with you there. He's just the same at home - he's never been able to shut up and listen to anyone else - or take it if he's in the wrong - he just storms off - it runs in the family - none of us can...

Facilitator: No - that's not what this is about at all. The reason why I wanted to talk to you was to tell you exactly what's been going on in school - how Michael has been operating and then to decide what I think we need to do if we're really going to give him the best possible chance of staying in school.

Mum:	So - he's going to get excluded again. What's he done now?
Facilitator:	Look - I'll put the cards on the table here. Michael is in some kind of trouble every single day. He sometimes can't get into the classroom because he's seen the teacher and then decided to have a go at them before they have a go at him. He does his level best to try and stop them teaching the lessons by running around the room, playing football, hitting other kids round the head, and then swearing out loud and constantly interrupting when the teacher has started explaining the lesson to the whole class. He refuses point blank to accept the three warnings system and if a teacher asks him to stop and listen he simply tells them to f... off and takes himself out of the room. If he's in one of the rooms in A block, he'll then go round the side of the building where he knows the teachers can still see him through the window and he'll take out a cigarette and smoke it.
Mum:	Like putting two fingers up at them I suppose - he's such a little bugger.
Facilitator:	The real problem here is that it is now a daily occurrence. He can't actually stay in class for more than a couple of minutes without some incident. He's had four fixed term exclusions now for his behaviour towards staff and the head of year has received 28 letters of complaint from other parents who say he's preventing their children from learning, three of which also accused him of making racist comments and bullying their children. Some of the teachers have complained that they don't want him in their classes anymore as he is preventing them from teaching and the other kids from learning. He really is on his last legs here, as the head of year and head of upper school have both said that the next exclusion is likely to be a permanent one.
Mum:	What? He won't be coming back here? What will happen to him then?
Facilitator:	Well, I can't be absolutely definite about the finer details, but what usually happens is that he'll be recommended for a place at the study centre.

Mum: But that's where all the nutters go and they're hardly in any lessons because I've often seen them wandering around town - even in our shop, where two of them were done for shoplifting. That's the last thing he needs. He's already halfway to becoming a little crook, and he'll just learn more of it if he goes there with that lot.

Facilitator: What he will learn is the core curriculum subjects for six hours a week, and then he'll have some activity-based afternoons, but as you say, it won't be full time schooling. There is also a waiting list at the moment, so it might be a few weeks before he could be offered a place anyway. What they also offer, which I would recommend, is some specialist counselling and support, and this is usually done because when kids have been permanently excluded they often get quite depressed and suffer from feelings of guilt and anger. To a certain extent, they feel labelled and of course very concerned that this will now really badly affect their future chances of getting a job as they'll be labelled as a trouble-maker who got kicked out of school. It can affect some kids for years and they need a lot of help to get over it.

Mum: I can't say it's not deserved, but that sounds really bad - like he'll have his cards marked for life - as if he'd been in prison or something.

Facilitator: Well, unfortunately, for some kids, in the worst case scenarios, that may well be true - but that isn't what we want to happen to Michael - which is why I wanted to talk to you. We want Michael to be able to stay in this school and to be able to get on and change his behaviour. It's not just me talking - I've spoken to the head of year, the head of upper school and many of his teachers, and all of us are prepared to try and help him out here...

Mum: It doesn't sound like he can be helped does it? I mean, it looks so bad

Facilitator: Look, if it really was that bad, they'd have permanently excluded him by now. They don't want to do it, or should I say, we don't, and that's why we're prepared to devote additional time and resources to him. We want to offer him a higher level of support and a special programme of skills teaching so that we can help him to change and help himself a bit more. This isn't me saying to you that we can work any magic here, but we can begin to make a difference. There is some hope that if he buys into this, and if we all work together to support him, then we can eliminate the threat of a permanent exclusion.

Mum: Well - I wasn't expecting that. I'm just so gobsmacked that you're going to do anything at all - well, since he's been such a little....

Facilitator: Right, we won't focus on what he's already done. Let me explain what I have in mind. What we're proposing to offer Michael is a place on a course called *School Survival*.

Mum: School what? What's that then?

Facilitator: Let me explain...

Communicating with other services

In running this course, the facilitator will want to be able to provide positive feedback to as many people as possible who can, in turn, respond in kind. If the students have a social worker or are being supported by an educational welfare officer, a mentor or a school councillor, then they should also receive regular feedback from the course facilitator. It may also be worthwhile considering having a 'guest slot' on the *School Survival* course and asking someone from the wider community (voluntary groups etc.) or a member of another service, to come in and talk to the group about what they do or even to teach a specific skill/ concept. An 'outsider' can also provide useful content which can then act as stimulation for future debate in the group. For example, someone from the Local Health Authority can talk about sexual health, drugs awareness and safety. Any guest speaker will, however, need to know what the aims and objectives of the group are, and will need to provide information that will further aid the students in terms of staying in school. The idea here is to disseminate knowledge and information that will help the student to stay in school – for example, this is how smoking a joint on a Wednesday might affect you on Thursday morning at school. Any guest speaker will need to work within the positive framework and existing ethos of the group.

Working in such a way is also particularly important if the facilitator decides to incorporate some kind of outdoor pursuits within the course context. The activity leader will need to be fully informed as to the aims of the course and be willing and able to work within the system outlined by the facilitator adopting the same philosophy, language and approach. This is vital if the outdoor pursuits are to really support and reinforce what is going on in the group back in the school. In order to achieve this, the facilitator would have to take quite an active part in the planning of any trips of this kind. In our experience, the majority of activity leaders have been delighted to receive such a good level of support and guidance. However, it is important to note that the level of success here is very much reliant upon the skills of the facilitator and the ways in which he presents and then handles the situation. As with any communication 'with others', the sensitivity, foresight, all round experience and social skills of the facilitator really do hold the key to success.

CONCEPT I
Looking For the Best Possible Outcome

Key concept

A central difficulty in working with students with emotional and behavioural difficulties is that of visualising and then effecting changes which will ensure the best possible outcome. The journey towards 'perfect behaviour' seems to be almost endless and the 'goal' can appear to be a long way away for those considering or attempting to achieve it. Rather than attempting to completely solve a problem or achieve perfection, it is suggested that students be given the opportunity to see and understand that some outcomes are better than others. Consequently the focus is upon identifying and taking smaller steps in order to achieve the better or more desired outcome, i.e. effect a change in behaviour. Students and teachers need to be able to identify the best possible outcome of any given situation and to also identify and make compromises along the way. The emphasis here is on the development of useful strategies and steps towards a solution for all involved – the approach is clearly solution-focused. De Shazer (1985) argues that such solutions can be formulated with a minimum focus upon the problem and its causation.

"There almost seems to be a logical break between problem talk and solution talk: the former does not automatically lead to the latter. Likewise, an extended discussion of the past will not necessarily lead to new ideas for solving problems in the present. Furthermore, for some clients, extended discussion of the past can actually be unhelpful, for example, where it leads to feelings of hopelessness".
Rhodes and Ajmal (1995), *Solution Focused Thinking in Schools* p.9

Target students will inevitably have experienced a huge amount of such negative feelings whilst trying to deal with the problem and when being targeted and focused upon as being the problem. Looking for the best possible outcome demands that teachers and students begin to gain a vision of 'life without the problem' (de Shazar 1998; Furman and Ahola 1992). It is, however, important to understand that this does not mean that this vision will be realised within a few weeks, but rather that the small steps will be identified to ensure that the student can begin to make the necessary journey behaviourally and at the same time feel, internally, that they are moving towards a better position. We cannot leap to perfection, but we can move towards a better place than current experience is giving us.

Consequently, solution-focused talk with the students needs to focus upon the movement of any situation from the negative to the positive.

Footprints

A very simple scale will illustrate this journey and aid the visualisation of the gradual movement along the scale as opposed to any miraculous (and unrealistic) leap.

Discussion will focus upon the movement of any situation towards the positive, whilst also highlighting how some of the choices that we make may well move a situation further towards the negative end of the scale. This process does not emphasise a 'right' way or a 'wrong' way of behaving or making choices, but rather presents the notion of positive choices leading to positive outcomes for the individuals concerned. Scaling activities such as the one provided help young people to visualise and then begin this positive movement.

Scaling

Visualising the movement towards the positive end of the scale may initially be further aided by breaking down the best possible outcome into three clearly defined steps:

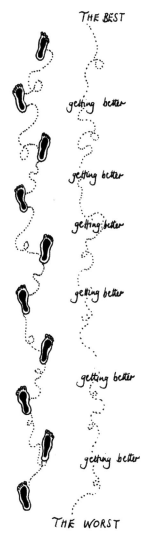

THE BEST

getting better

getting better

getting better

getting better

getting better

getting better

THE WORST

- The best possible outcome in the short-term
- The best possible outcome in the medium-term
- The best possible outcome in the long-term

With each step, students can also be encouraged to identify the smaller steps that they may have to take in order to eventually achieve the best possible outcome in the long-term, alongside the resources and support structures that they may need to use in order to proceed on this journey. Essentially, they need to be able to make the choices that will move them in the right direction.

The Scaling Activity

Name _____

Year Group _____

The Scale – Highlight where you are now.

⓿ ❶ ❷ ❸ ❹ ❺ ❻ ❼ ❽ ❾ 10

Questions to Answer

1) Where am I now?

2) Why

3) Where would I like to be?

4) How can I get there? What do my targets need to be?

Wish List

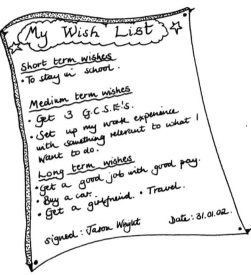

Illustrative script
What is the best outcome? The conversation

Teacher:	What we need to do today Michael, is to think about how you can make the movement along the scale - how you can move on towards achieving a better outcome for yourself. What do you think the positive end of the scale looks like for you? How would things be different or better?
Michael:	Well, I'd be in class all the time and I wouldn't be in trouble in lessons for answering back. I suppose the teachers wouldn't be picking on me all the time - like saying I was bad, and I'd find some work easier and get better grades.
Teacher:	Where else in your life might there be a difference?
Michael:	Well I suppose my Mum would get off my back if I wasn't in trouble.
Teacher:	Okay - that sounds great - you can really see where you'd like to be - what about getting to that point? How close are you to getting there?
Michael:	Miles away.
Teacher:	Right. So what is the first smallest step towards that position? What is the smallest thing you could do to help things get better?
Michael:	I don't know...I suppose I could not answer back and just keep quiet, but that would be hard because other people don't...it's just that they don't get caught like me.

Teacher: Well, I think we need to exclude them from the equation - you need to focus on what's good for YOU. But I think you might have hit the nail on the head there - you started out by saying 'I could not answer back' and that's just where I want to stop you - it's clear really that this is going to be down to you Michael, but it's really hard to change overnight. We need to look at what will help you to not answer back. The trouble is, in the end you're the only one that can control yourself. What do you think?

Michael: I suppose so...

Teacher: Let's break it down a bit. We need to get back down the scale a and break this into smaller steps. Let's think about what your best outcome in the short-term would be. What do you want to change in the next few days or weeks? Let's make it something that would be the best outcome just for now.

Michael: Hmmm...

Teacher: What could we see that would be different?

Michael: I think I could try to stay in class and not get chucked out after three minutes.

Teacher: Why is it three minutes?

Michael: That's normally how long it takes for the teachers to make up their minds that I'm being rude.

Teacher: Well, what is it that you're doing in those three minutes?

Michael: I suppose I thump the table and throw my bag down. I just get moody, because I know I can't do the work.

Teacher: Always?

Michael: Well, not exactly...but most of the time.

Teacher: Well...if you didn't thump the table and throw your bag down, you might have a better chance of surviving the lesson. If you manage to change that initial behaviour what would be a good target to move towards?

Michael: Well, I suppose staying in the lesson for longer, like 10 minutes.

Teacher: Ten minutes? 20? 30? What would be a realistic goal for now?

Michael: Ten I suppose.

Teacher: Great. Let's go with that. It'll be your first step - your first best possible outcome on the way to the best one of all.

Teaching the concept

<u>Conversation</u>
Initially, it is a good idea to focus upon belief systems and to ask the students to reflect and articulate their own views. Clearly, if these are entirely negative, then it may not be possible to achieve a best possible outcome. If you think that school really is a waste of time and effort, then it will be virtually impossible to move forwards. The beliefs we have and the choices we make will always impact upon our behaviours and their outcomes. The central question at the start of this topic should be as follows: Does your belief system get you a best possible outcome? Does it move you further in the positive direction on the scale? Also, as part of this journey, it will be necessary to constantly ask the question: you have done that/made that choice – will it give you a better outcome? Again, this is adopting the solution-focused approach whilst continually demanding that students not only reflect upon their choices and behaviours, but also take responsibility for the outcomes and achieve a state of internal control. The questioning should always remain positive – not asking if this is the worst or best way to do it, but simply asking will it give you the best possible outcome?

<u>Body building</u>
This is a simple example of moving towards an end goal in small steps. When we want to loose weight, get fitter or change the way our body looks, it doesn't happen overnight. The body builder doesn't expect to meet with perfection a few days after deciding that he or she wants to change. It can be

useful to have pictures of sportsmen and women, body builders or 'beautiful people' to illustrate the conversation. A follow on activity is to plan a training regime for an athlete for a year leading up to the Olympics – it doesn't have to be physiologically accurate, it must just represent and illustrate an idea of moving slowly towards a better position, in small steps, over a period of time.

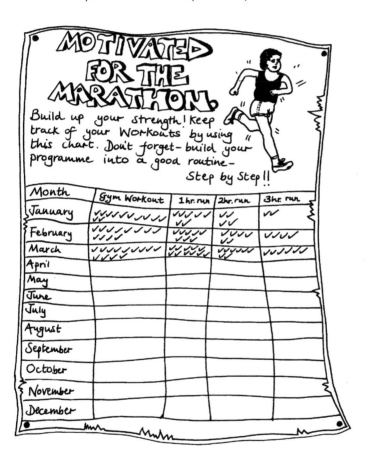

Snakes and ladders

This form of questioning and problem solving can be practised and reinforced via a snakes and ladders board game. How do you know if this choice will enable you to go up the ladder? Why will another choice result in slipping backwards down the snake? How can you move forward again in order to gain the best possible outcome? The students can devise and make their own versions of this game and include the problems that they may encounter/have encountered, and the choices that they have.

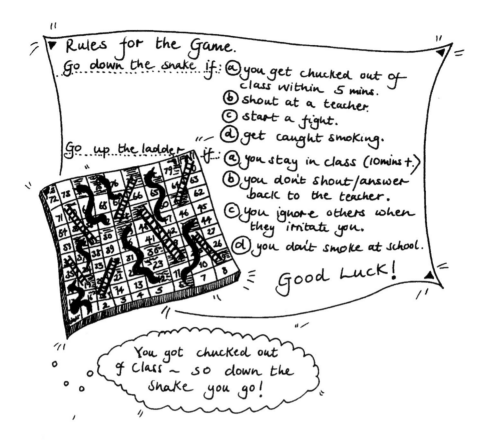

Constructing and playing this type of game should aid in reinforcing the distinction between positive and negative choices and enable the students to visualise, more effectively, where they want to get to and what they want to achieve for themselves.

Consequences – a question of sport?
The fact that our behaviours have consequences is central to the underlying philosophy of this approach and it is essential that students are encouraged to understand and accept this fact. A useful strategy to introduce and reinforce this concept is the 'what happened next?' game (as seen in the TV programme *A Question of Sport*). Students can be presented with a range of situations or they can make up their own scenarios. These can be 'acted out' or simply discussed around the table. Situations can be recorded on small cards/ pieces of paper and then passed around the group with each student answering the question 'What happened next?'

Alternatively, it may be useful (if time-consuming) to video a range of scenes from a variety of soaps and films and to use these in order to teach this concept. Students can ask the same question of each scene and although this may be quite an undertaking, it is really worth the effort. Not only will you have a re-useable resource but it will also be one that will actively engage the students right from the start as it can be formulated to clearly reflect youth culture.

Diagrams and choice points

Using simple diagrams can also reinforce this notion of making choices in order to ensure the best possible outcome.

The choice point is the point at which the student can choose to respond/ act in a way which will either ensure a positive or a negative outcome. They can be encouraged to reflect upon their choices and distinguish between outcomes – which one would really be the best for me? Which would be best for me in the short-, medium- and long-term?

The choice point may also prompt a chain reaction and students can attempt to formulate their own list of consequences – either in discussion around the table or in a simple flow diagram. For example:

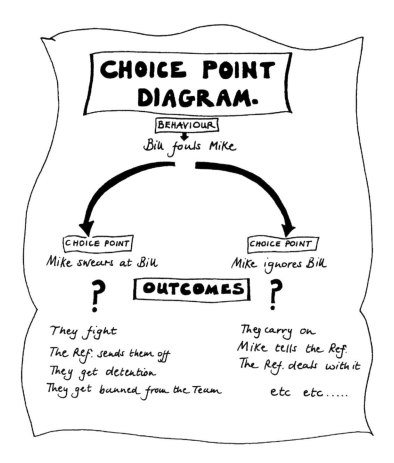

At each point of such a chain reaction, there will be a choice that the individual could have made. The students can be encouraged to identify these choices and to highlight those which might have resulted in a more positive outcome. They can also write/formulate an alternative/'positive' chain reaction for the same scenario.

Making it Real – A Negative Chain Reaction

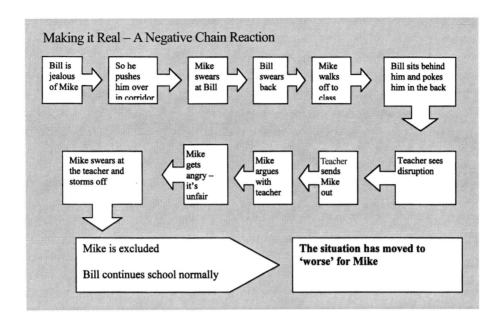

It is also useful to provide the students with opportunities to role-play such scenarios. The facilitator could take on the role of the teacher and act out the scenario with each student or with the group as a whole.

For example, one scene may involve the student coming in to the lesson late and immediately responding in an off-hand way to the teacher's initial reprimand. The students and course facilitator can assess and determine at which stage in the scene the choice point has arisen, and then discuss or act out both the negative and more positive response. Using focus questions can help here, such as:

- What way could this go?
- How could the student react?
- How could the teacher react?

Students can also attempt to devise three possible ways in which the scene may develop, and then rank these in terms of outcomes.

P.S.

- Students identify time of stress and are encouraged to explore their reactions

- Use of role-play to explore how stress can effect choices and subsequent outcomes

- One of the areas that students initially find difficult is 'talking about ourselves'. It is important to address this issue early on by devising explicit exercises that encourage a more fluid dialogue. It is important not to underestimate the difficulties that some pupils may have in talking about themselves, or others, in a positive light. Some of the areas addressed might include:
  - Talking about me
  - Talking about you
  - Saying positive things
  - Using 'I' statements
  - The power I have when receiving and giving praise
  - Listening to advice and guidance

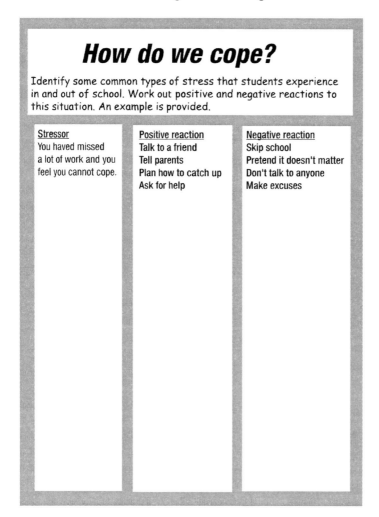

How do we cope?

Identify some common types of stress that students experience in and out of school. Work out positive and negative reactions to this situation. An example is provided.

Stressor	Positive reaction	Negative reaction
You haved missed a lot of work and you feel you cannot cope.	Talk to a friend Tell parents Plan how to catch up Ask for help	Skip school Pretend it doesn't matter Don't talk to anyone Make excuses

CONCEPT 2
Looking at Behaviour – Teaching the Students to Analyse and Reflect

Key concept

This concept is essentially about developing the student's ability to talk about their behaviour and the behaviour of others. When behaviour is discussed in most contexts it carries with it a great deal of emotional baggage. This does not necessarily have to be so. However, it is often the emotions associated with behaviour that block any positive movement forward when trying to develop more positive behavioural responses.

It is also important when looking specifically at behaviour to realise that for the student (and for adults) it is generally the external and observable behaviour that will result in the negative outcomes – students don't get excluded for thinking bad thoughts, they get excluded for acting them out. Feelings and thoughts can, to a certain extent, be held back, hidden and remain unobserved by those around us. Behaviour, on the other hand, is what others see us do. It can be observed, analysed and judged. It's what gets us into trouble!

However, it is important to point out that teaching these survival skills will not result in angelic behaviour. We do not expect the students to behave like little angels, but rather, to show behaviours to others that won't get them into trouble.

Students need to be empowered to think that they can change and that they are not expected to be 'perfect'. Also, it is crucial to reinforce the fact that just because you

may behave 'badly' at times, this does not mean that you are a bad or evil person. This message needs to be continually reinforced in order to counteract negative self-perceptions that may have been reinforced over a long period of time. The message should not be read 'you're a naughty boy and intrinsically evil', but rather 'your behaviour is not what we, or you for that matter, want'.

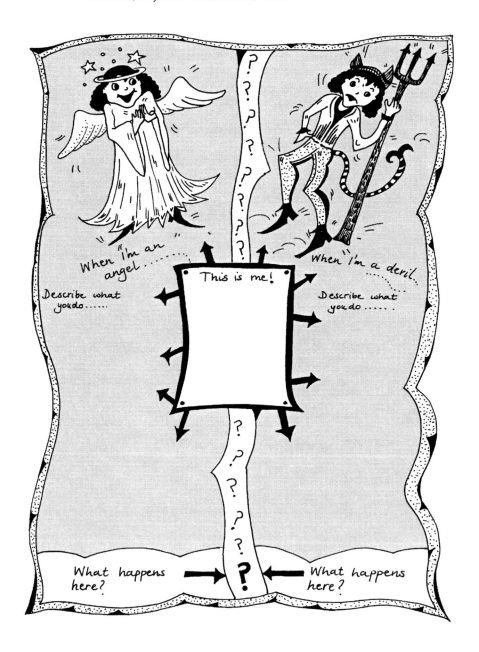

It is essential that this latter message is what the students receive and that they fully understand and internalise it. This message does not threaten self-esteem and subsequently allows them to look at their own behaviours and analyse them – almost as a third party. Talking about behaviour in this way is essentially a safe activity – safe-guarding the self-esteem of those involved. We can talk about the behaviour, as being distinct from the person, even though we know there is a connection there. This idea can be illustrated for the students in a number of ways. The important thing is always to help develop the students vision of their behaviour as a specific part of them which they can discuss in the third person.

Students can quickly understand the functions of this kind of safe, 'protecting inner self' talk, and move from it to be able to develop the analytical and observational skills that effect positive changes and outcomes. As shown by the '?' marks in the last diagram, it is important to develop the student's understanding of what are the causes of these different behaviours.

Students need to be able to describe behaviour in an extremely objective way and to develop strong observational skills. They also need to develop and use a descriptive vocabulary in order to talk about their behaviour in fine detail, i.e. 'he came in through the door' needs to develop into 'he put his hand on the door and pushed it open - it opened slowly and he then took his hand away'. Encouraging such fine detail can be an aid to accurate recall and the acceptance of the consequences of solving the problem 'next time'.

Looking at behaviour can be promoted as a concept by making reference to the following points:

- Behaviour needs to be described objectively with no use of emotive language. E.g. 'He came into the room and sat down. As he sat down he threw his bag on the floor'; rather than 'He came into the room in a bad mood'
- The sequence of behaviour is important. Precursors, catalysts and triggers for behaviour need to be identified and then associated with a variety of behaviours and their outcomes and consequences
- It is useful when discussing behaviours to be objectively identifying patterns over time. E.g. 'Do you realise that in the first five minutes of every lesson you always ask to go to the toilet? Why is this so and how does it affect your behaviour in the rest of the lesson?'
- Analysis of interactions also needs to be included as this allows students to make the links between actions and behaviours. E.g. 'Joe did…which led Paul to behave like this…'
- It is also worthwhile exploring the physical environment and context and its impact upon behaviour. E.g. 'If you sit next to the window the teacher might think you are not working because you are looking out of the window'

Illustrative script
Describing the behaviour – the conversation

Teacher:	So Diane, tell me what happened? What did you do?
Diane:	Miss Price was in a bad mood so she picked on me and I told her to f... off and walked out because I didn't need to put up with it.
Teacher:	Okay - let's go back a bit. How did you know Miss Price was in a bad mood? What did she do?
Diane:	She shouted.
Teacher:	When - before or after you'd sat down?
Diane:	Before.
Teacher:	Why was that?
Diane:	Because I walked in stroppy.

Teacher:	What do you mean? What were you doing?
Diane:	I came into the class in a huff and I didn't look at her when she said hello. Then I threw my bag onto the table and sat down. When I sat down it was heavy and I kicked the table leg. Then she shouted at me.
Teacher:	What did she say?
Diane:	What's wrong with you?
Teacher:	How did she say it?
Diane:	Not loud - like she was worried.
Teacher:	So what did you do?
Diane:	I rolled my eyes to say what is it to you. She was making the others look at me and I felt stupid. Then she said 'you don't have to do that'! I looked at her and said 'yes I do - just leave me alone!'. Then she went red in the face and told me that I was being rude and she wouldn't put up with it. I told her to mind her own business and I kicked my table towards her and said, 'Get off my back'. Then she said I should get out of the class straight away. So I said I would get out and she could just f... off. I kicked the desk over and picked up my bag and went out of the room.
Teacher:	Now we've got more of the fine detail. So, let's think about this again and try and work out what you could have done to get a better outcome. Where did you need to make a different choice?

Teaching the concept

<u>Conversation</u>

In order to prompt students to develop accurate and descriptive accounts, it is important to ask the 'right' questions. These might include some of the following:

- If I was the teacher and I had walked into the classroom when you were behaving like that, what would I have seen?
- If there was a video camera in the classroom and it had been used to film what was going on, what would I actually see when I played it back and watched the whole thing?
- What did your friends see you doing?

Video reflections – what I actually saw

An effective way of developing the student's observational skills and associated language is to give them opportunities to watch well chosen scenes from TV programmes (soap operas are especially effective). They should then describe, to each other, what they actually saw. Initially, these video clips can be as short as 20 seconds and the students can then be asked to try and record at least 10 things that happened in this very short space of time. In this way, the focus is on the minute details – the flicker of an eye, a click of the fingers, a slight turn of the head, a look of fear or anger and so on. In effect, students are encouraged to begin to further analyse social interactions and to see the connections between these and specific behaviours and outcomes. Again, the focus is on the consequences of behaviour.

In being able to accurately describe what someone did (actions) the student should also be able to identify how this affected others and whether or not different choices could have been made in order to achieve a better outcome.

Body language

In describing behaviours, students will also need to be able to understand and evaluate body language. How do we know when someone is feeling got at, angry, afraid, put down, or out of control? What happens to their face, shoulders, fists, arms and tone of voice? The notion of empathy comes into play here and, of course, the essential requirement of developing emotional literacy. The students need to be encouraged to articulate and understand how and why they feel as they do in different situations, and how their feelings and behaviours impact upon others. Observing how others look and sound, and analysing such observations, can begin to develop such skills and this fact is well supported by research (Greenberg & Kusche (1993), Elias & Clabby (1992)) which shows that students need to develop adequate social and emotional skills in order to be able to modify their own behaviour.

Looking at body language and developing the language to accurately describe it and interpret it can be done via role play, observing others (and oneself) in 'real' life and by watching and analysing a range of video clips and resources. Building up a bank of video resources which presents a wide variety of behaviours and emotions (not simply the uncomfortable ones like anger or the acts of aggression that are often associate with loss of temper) is extremely helpful here. It is important to include situations which present characters experiencing and doing things that model positive outcomes, and which include positive and pleasurable emotions such as love, happiness and excitement. This is necessary in order to ensure that the emotional vocabulary and descriptive language learnt and used covers both the positive and negative life experiences. Clearly, it is also important for students to be able to develop these skills whilst analysing and reflecting upon positives. A continual /endless focus on negative behaviours will only teach the associated negative vocabulary, and will also impact negatively upon the student's self-esteem.

Owning it – it's your behaviour, you own it
Work with the students also needs to specifically state that the behaviours they are learning to describe and analyse belong to them. Asking the question 'who does the behaviour belong to?' can promote an interesting debate and essentially helps to reinforce the concept of internal control – it is your behaviour, it belongs to you and no one else. This means that the student can't 'blame' anyone else for it. They are also able to change the behaviour if they want to. What is important is to emphasise that the process of change doesn't imply perfection. Continually highlight that it is the behaviour that needs to change and not the student as a person. Again, this is the notion of disliking the behaviour and not the child. When students are asked to talk about their behaviour and listen to others do the same, this can be perceived by them as an attack upon their self-esteem and confidence. Talking about behaviour in the third person, as we propose, should help to combat this problem to some extent. Also, the more that students are encouraged to observe, reflect and talk, the more their confidence will build up, allowing them to be more objective and less confrontational. It is essential that the facilitator makes absolutely sure that the group environment they have created allows for the development of such skills and confidence and certainly doesn't undermine or damage the self-concept of the students involved.

Reflecting on other's views
Further discussion also needs to focus on these questions:

- What does my behaviour say?
- How do other people interpret my behaviour?
- How do I interpret other's behaviour?

In order to effectively answer the first two questions, it will be necessary to elicit the views of those who teach the students. However, it will be essential to ensure that these members of staff are actually speaking the same language. For example, if teachers are sending incident slips back to the head of year then these need to detail exactly what the problem behaviour is. They must make making use of the descriptive language that students are being encouraged to develop and use. If the student knows exactly what it is that the teacher feels is wrong, then they will be in a better position to change it.

"Tony was rude and verbally abusive"
is not always as helpful as:
"Tony came into the room with an angry look on his face, he scowled at me and made farting noises throughout my introduction to the lesson. These got louder and louder until the other students couldn't hear me. I asked him to stop three times and he ignored me".

Naturally, the second option takes longer to write, but it certainly enables the student and facilitator to identify exactly what the undesirable behaviours were, and so enables more accurate targets to be set for the future.

What makes my behaviour happen?
Throughout the *School Survival* course, students will be encouraged to analyse and question their own perceptions, belief systems, behaviour patterns, skills, desires and needs, and also those of their peers and adults, in all their social contexts. The self-questioning process will be continual:

- How do I perceive others?
- How do others perceive various situations – at home/ school/ socially?
- How do others perceive me? How can I be sure? What signals do they give me? Why?
- What do I believe?
- What are my political, moral and spiritual views?
- What are the behaviour patterns I've developed, and why have they developed in this way?
- What skills and strengths do I have and how do I know that I have them?
- What needs do I have – educationally, emotionally, financially, socially, spiritually?
- What are my desires – what do I really want now – in the short-, medium- and long-term?

Students will become aware that it is these perceptions, beliefs, patterns, skills, needs and desires that all feed into their behaviour. These are the things that prompt and underlie our conduct – both in ourselves and to others. It is also these areas that the students will be working on in order to change and gain more positive outcomes. This process is absolutely central to the *School Survival* philosophy. Initially, the fact that these things feed into our behaviour, and that the consequences and outcomes result from it, can be presented to students in a simple diagram as follows.

<u>Feeding into behaviour</u>

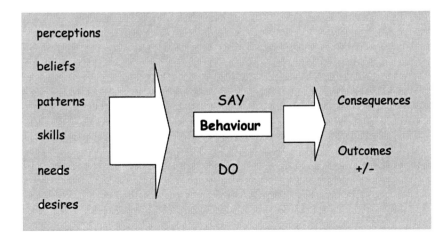

This will allow the discussion to begin regarding each of the behaviour aspects outlined above, but the facilitator/teacher will need to continually return to these throughout the intervention. If talking about behaviour is central and essential, then so is being aware of where this behaviour comes from.

Modelling

A further aid to developing the descriptive language for behaviour is to encourage the students to actually model/ 'act out' their behaviour to the facilitator/teacher, i.e. show me exactly what you did – step by step. This again allows for a focus on the physical movements – what did you do with your hands, your face, your voice, your body? This process clearly demands a high level of sensitivity and skill from the facilitator/teacher, but it is an extremely powerful tool and well worth persevering with, as it also allows the students to 'act out' or model what would have been a more positive behaviour.

As always, remember: "What could you have done in order to gain the best possible outcome here? Show me!".

Using the tape recorder/video

The 'Feeding into Behaviour' diagram illustrates that much of the students' behaviour, whether it leads to a positive or a negative outcome, is dependant on what they say. What comes out of your mouth in a confrontational situation, or even as part of your everyday, 'normal' social interactions, can be crucial in terms of consequences and outcomes. Students need to be encouraged to reflect upon their verbal interactions and use of language in order to assess the impact that these may have on others, alongside identifying the need to change or modify the way that they talk and what they say.

Using a tape recorder is particularly helpful for this process and, like using the video, it's a lot of fun. Both resources enable the students to respond very quickly and the immediate quality of these media ensure that no time is wasted and that students have access to on the spot feedback. Students can roleplay/act out a variety of situations which can be video-ed/taped and then analysed in terms of exactly what happened, why things happened, what the causes and consequences were, and how everyone involved looked, sounded and felt.

Further analysis can explore how the consequences were a direct result of these behaviours. Alternative behaviours can be 'acted out', i.e. those which will ensure positive consequences, and it may also be helpful to use the video within the classroom context itself – not simply to record the student's behaviours and verbal interactions, but perhaps to also focus upon the teacher.

Students need to be encouraged to further develop empathy and to see things from another's perspective. They may focus upon a range of questions in order to do this:
- What is the teacher doing? (physically – body language, tone of voice, eye contact, movement)
- Why? What is this in response to?
- How do you know how he/ she feels at each point in the lesson? How can you tell? What are the signals?
- How does he/she respond to an 'unwanted' piece of behaviour? What does he/she do?
- What is the outcome in the short-, medium- and long-term in this lesson?
- What else do you think the teacher could do? Why?
- What would you do in the teacher's position? Why?
- How would you cope with the teacher who responded to you in this way? What would you do next and why?

P.S.
- Aggressive/passive/assertive distinctions – teaching and role modelling these – what works and why? What doesn't work and why?

- Behaviour/feelings diaries – recording both on a daily basis and then analysing the context of these in order to find a more positive way of behaving (and feeling) in the future

- How about using cartoons to caricature what their, and others, behaviours can look like. A good approach to this is to compile a guide to 'Reading Body Language', perhaps aimed at the alien market

- Students can write letters to their behaviour as this may help the student visualise it in the third person

- Students can do a survey about their behaviour – what do others see?

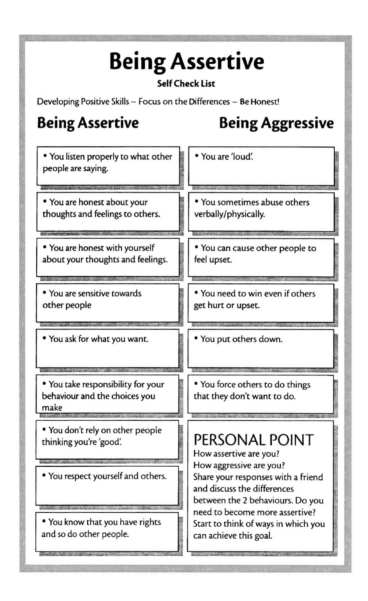

Being Assertive

Self Check List

Developing Positive Skills – Focus on the Differences – Be Honest!

Being Assertive

- You listen properly to what other people are saying.

- You are honest about your thoughts and feelings to others.

- You are honest with yourself about your thoughts and feelings.

- You are sensitive towards other people

- You ask for what you want.

- You take responsibility for your behaviour and the choices you make

- You don't rely on other people thinking you're 'good'.

- You respect yourself and others.

- You know that you have rights and so do other people.

Being Aggressive

- You are 'loud'.

- You sometimes abuse others verbally/physically.

- You can cause other people to feel upset.

- You need to win even if others get hurt or upset.

- You put others down.

- You force others to do things that they don't want to do.

PERSONAL POINT
How assertive are you?
How aggressive are you?
Share your responses with a friend and discuss the differences between the 2 behaviours. Do you need to become more assertive? Start to think of ways in which you can achieve this goal.

Work with a partner and try to identify all the strategies and skills you could use.

CONCEPT 3
Using Targets

Key concept

School Survival is an attempt to be as efficient as possible in the way that it addresses and then attempts to change behaviour. In order to measure and ensure this efficiency, a system of target setting is used. We are by no means the first to suggest that those experiencing behaviour problems at school be set targets. But unlike targets that represent an ultimatum – meet these or you're out', targets are used in this programme to focus support through a planned process of change.

The use of targets offers the following attributes:

- Targets can break down what may be seen as a huge task into small steps in the right direction
- They offer something concrete for the students to work on
- We are able to measure whether or not interventions are working
- We (and perhaps more importantly the students) are able to see progress
- Constraints such as time, resources and reality can be taken into account
- They aid and are part of the analysis of a situation, often helping to identify the way forward
- Targets help communicate expectations to all

The use of targets will need to be SMART:

S PECIFIC

MEASUREABLE

A CHIEVEABLE

R EALISTIC

T IME CONSTRAINED

Targets will need to be identified and worked upon at every stage of
the course. However, in addition to these principles of target setting,
targets will need to encourage an overall vision of the journey as set
out in Concept 1 – looking for the best possible outcomes. Students
will need to have some idea of their longer-term goal or target, and
where they hope to get to by the end of the course, but they will also
need to identify the steps that they need to take along the way. This
will also mean identifying short-term and medium-term targets which
are directly linked to the envisaged best possible outcomes at
these stages.

Clearly, these targets will need to be formulated with each individual
student at some point near the start of the course. The target setting
process is essential in subsequently allowing each student to measure
his success at the end of the course. However, the targets will also
enable the facilitator to measure the success of his own inputs. Was
the content really appropriate? Did the ideas, strategies and
interventions really work for the student? How successful was I in
ensuring the best possible outcome for them?

When we say that targets will need to be specific, this is so that when
the student meets a target, this success will really have a
disproportionate effect and impact upon them and those around
them. By carefully analysing the student's behaviour, the facilitator will
need to identify the very small change that is needed in order to get
the greatest change in behaviour. For example, many of the students
we have worked with are set a target of arriving to the lesson on time

or within the first five minutes of the lesson. This is because if they **do** arrive for the lesson within the first five minutes, then their chances of surviving that lesson are massively increased. Arriving later than this would inevitably result in conflict and stress for all involved.

An initial problem encountered at this early stage is that, when setting the first targets, the student may be less skilled or completely unskilled in terms of both understanding and describing their own behaviours in the detailed, objective and third person fashion as outlined previously. Consequently, we suggest that targets are not set within the first week, but rather that students are simply encouraged to think about what or where they may like to change. Targets can then be set around the second or third week (as appropriate).

Subsequently, these targets will be continually referred to within the group and each student will know exactly what everyone else's targets are. Matter of fact questioning of each pupil in every session needs to be commonplace and overt: 'What is your target? What is _____'s target?' 'How are we doing?' The fact that this kind of discussion takes place within a safe, secure and very matter of fact context, means that the students will become empowered and negative feelings and effects upon self-esteem will be reduced. The group itself is intended to form a support base for students – a place in which they can help and support each other to develop positive skills, both social and emotional, that will also allow them to achieve their goals.

Illustrative script

Teacher:	So what do you feel that your overall goal - your 'big' target should be Gemma?
Gemma:	Well - I want to go to college in the future to do a course in plumbing. My Dad's a plumber and I go and help him on Saturdays so I know a lot already and he said I'd be good at the job - plus I'd be employed by myself so I wouldn't have to get up early and I could work late instead - which my Dad says would be good.
Teacher:	What a good start. You seem to be clear. It's a sham e that one of your key subjects will be maths.
Gemma:	I know. It stinks.

Teacher:	Okay - but you will need to get it, won't you, if you're going into plumbing.
Gemma:	Yeah.
Teacher:	So, let's think this all through a bit and draw it out. I'll do the drawing - here's a ladder and you're right at the bottom here. Now, what I think we need to do is work out the targets that you need to meet in order to get up to the top of the ladder.
Gemma:	Okay.
Teacher:	Right - let's start at the bottom. When you've been describing your behaviour to me it seems that a lot of your rows with the teachers are a direct result of you going into class late and then getting lippy with them when they tell you off for being late. Am I right?
Gemma:	Yeah - So the first one should be that I get there on time.
Teacher:	But what is stopping you from getting there on time?
Gemma:	Just hanging about with my friends.
Teacher:	What are the choices here?
Gemma:	I know, I know!
Teacher:	So if you are on time to lessons, it may be the first step to stopping the big rows. If you're there at the start, your behaviour is saying something to the teacher -like you are ready for work.
Gemma:	Even if I'm not really?
Teacher:	But it will look as if you are, and you can show that you are in your body language by facing them and giving them eye contact when they're talking to the whole class - okay?
Gemma:	Yeah - I know what you mean - if I can do that, it's like two targets, and then I can stay in for the whole lesson and not get kicked out.
Teacher:	Well, that could be your medium-term target - what do you think?
Gemma:	Okay - I'll have a go.

Teaching the concept

<u>Future basing</u>

This strategy encourages students to visualise where they will be in five years time, i.e. their own preferred future. This visualising helps them see how and where they will be, but also allows them to **feel** how they will be. Sufficient time should be spent exploring as many aspects of their future life as possible.

Once this has been established, they can work backwards, identifying the small steps they will have to take on the way, until they reach their present position as students in high school. This approach encourages the recognition of the consequences of behaviours and the choice points that will arise for each individual. There is also a sense of flow and movement here. Life itself does not stand still but is continually moving forward and changing for all of us. The strategy enables students to articulate long-term targets and goals, and the short- and medium-term targets they will need to meet along the way in order to get to where they want to be in five years time.

<u>Short-term targets</u>

The more desperate student who is struggling and finding the school context extremely difficult will require immediate short-term targets – particularly those that are linked to rewards. It is vital that the student begins to experience some success and the target that is initially set (and subsequent ones) needs to be something that they can actually achieve. There is absolutely no point in setting short-term targets that the student won't be able to meet. They cannot afford to fail and

clearly need to be set up for success. Short-term targets need to be SMART with an emphasis on the **A**chievable. They should be continually adjusted via incremental steps. A useful way of explaining this process to students is via illustrations of a series of steps, a staircase, ladder, or a brick wall. It is important that they can visualise themselves moving up, step by step, and that the targets allow them to do this.

<u>Time factors</u>

All targets need to have a time limit set upon them – whether these are long-, medium- or short-term. For those targets that are short-term, this time limit can be extremely tight and targets may have to be set on a daily or sessional basis. Students can then measure their success within this varying timeframe. For example, if the target concerns keeping up in lessons, a student may have success throughout the morning, but may find the task more difficult towards the end of the day. Breaking up the day into three separate sessions would allow them to experience success for two to three sessions at least, and this is preferable to attempting to measure success right at the end of the day.

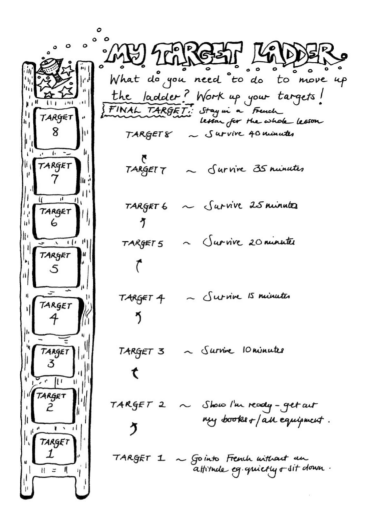

MY TARGET LADDER

What do you need to do to move up the ladder? Work up your targets!

FINAL TARGET: Stay in a French lesson for the whole lesson

TARGET 8 ~ Survive 40 minutes

TARGET 7 ~ Survive 35 minutes

TARGET 6 ~ Survive 25 minutes

TARGET 5 ~ Survive 20 minutes

TARGET 4 ~ Survive 15 minutes

TARGET 3 ~ Survive 10 minutes

TARGET 2 ~ Show I'm ready – get out my books & / all equipment.

TARGET 1 ~ Go into French without an attitude eg. quietly & sit down.

The student may well have had an excellent morning, started off reasonably well in the afternoon session, but then blown it towards the end of the day. To then say 'you've failed and not met your target today' would present another attack upon his/her self-esteem, and such an approach doesn't encourage a renewed effort the next day. At all times, it is vital to consider what the student can actually manage, and where he may be most successful. It may well be that the student who manages to keep up for the morning session should initially be given the target just for those sessions, so that he is assured of success in the first instance. This is what target setting should be about – ensuring success and helping to eliminate failure.

During the initial stages of the course, building up the student's self-esteem, so that they feel they can successfully change their behaviour pattern, is absolutely crucial. It is therefore the adult's responsibility to set REAL targets where the student WILL NOT FAIL. But it is also important that the targets are real in the eyes of the student. If the targets are perceived as being made up or too easy, then the accompanying feelings of success when a target is met will not be one of the benefits.

Using the group supportively
As previously stated, each student within the group will have access to and knowledge of each other's targets. Developing a supportive, empathetic ethos is essential, and making use of each student's developing skills in order to support their peers will have the added bonus of reinforcing self-respect and self-esteem. Students will be developing self-reflection skills, observation skills and the vocabulary to objectively describe their behaviours and those of others.

The facilitator/teacher can pose a range of questions that will encourage the students to actively support each other openly:

What was 'X' doing when he came into the classroom?
- So do you think he met his target?
- What would he have needed to do in order to meet his target?
- What do you think you could do to help him reach his target?
- Do you think his target is realistic?
- Is his target too easy?

Peer support of this kind is extremely powerful and is also a useful means of transferring the work of the group and the work done by the group into the classroom. For example, the little nod or wink from a friend who knows that you have a specific target to meet that day can be the prompt that ensures you make the right choice, successfully meet your target, and so achieve the best possible outcome at that moment in time.

Members of the group can, in fact, act almost as a kind of circle of friends for each other, showing understanding, acknowledging and supporting each other's needs, and celebrating each other's successes.

As Ted Hughes writes:
"In an intact group the pool of shared understandings is like a shared bank account of the group wealth, it does not diminish by being spent. Rather, the more lavishly it is circulated, the greater inner wealth and security each single member feels to have". (1994)

Using the school discipline framework/behaviour code

When setting targets it is useful to refer to and make use of the systems already in existence in the school context. For example, if students receive detentions for not handing in homework, or for unwanted behaviour in class, then the target can make specific reference to this – I'll only get one detention this week. If the disciplinary framework makes use of time out for students who refuse to co-operate in class, then the target may read 'I'll only use time out twice this week – maximum! You are setting targets that have some relation to the 'real' world and its expectations.

Such targets should then allow the facilitator to show school staff that the student is improving and making an effort in terms of the student's success criteria for behaviour. When the student gets fewer detentions, is excluded from class less often, or receives fewer minus points or conduct slips, whatever the disciplinary measures used, it will be possible to highlight his success against these systems, and this is a powerful tool. When the students themselves can see their success in terms of the school structures, this is a powerful reinforcement that they can be and, to some extent, are being, included in that system. Their success will also begin to build any broken bridges with the rest of the school, i.e. beginning to repair any damaged relationships with peers outside the group and school staff.

Addressing motivation

Throughout the *School Survival* programme, targets can be used in order to address student motivation. Being motivated is essential in order to achieve success. The students will need to actively participate in this target setting process. Depending on the make-up of the group and the personalities and abilities of the students involved, targets can continually be re-formulated and adjusted to ensure and increase motivation. This may mean that targets are directly related to home and outside of school – particularly if the motivation of the group needed further bolstering at any stage.

<u>Using rewards to motivate</u>
Students who are likely to be targeted by the *School Survival* intervention may well have previously experienced little positive feedback, so it is essential that this is addressed within the course. Obviously this can take the form of positive verbal praise, but it may well be necessary to link more tangible rewards to their set targets. It is vital that these rewards are perceived, by the students, as genuine. This will only be the case when they are offered or given within a genuine relationship – a sticker from an adult that evidently cares about the student and his school experience will hold far more meaning for the student than a publicly awarded certificate from someone with whom they do not have a positive relationship. A reward is really just an acknowledgement of something the student themselves would value or learn to value. It is vital to remember this fact in order to mitigate against giving superficial or inappropriate rewards.

P.S.

- Use of brief therapy interviews to set targets

- Get pupils to set targets for each other. In practice this would mean that in the group of weekly agreed targets, their peers may set one of these targets. Often this target can encourage an element of competition that may be useful, depending upon the nature of the group

- It is possible to develop a game where each student within the group attempts, in turn, to remember the targets for the others in the group

- As part of the review of the week it is possible for the group to assess whether or not an individual has met their targets

- Secret signs: what signals can pupils give each other in class to make someone who is making poor choices calm down and switch into a better choice mode?

Part 2

a) The Miracle Question

Imagine that you go to bed tonight and a miracle happens - someone or something waves a magic wand over you and all your problems and difficulties are solved.

You wake up to a 'Perfect Day' at home and at school.

What is different? Have a THINK. How does your day begin and then go on?

Talk through what happens on this miraculous day.

> I get up and my Mum tells me to have a shower. She's in a good mood and makes a fry-up. I go to school on my new motor bike and my mates all see it and they are impressed.
> when I go into class the teacher says 'Hello- how are things going?'
> I am good at my work and get loads of credits. I don't get into trouble.
> I have pizza for lunch and it's P.E. all afternoon.
> I don't have any hoework and I can watch whatever I want on T.V. and we have cable. I can go to bed when i want and Mum is in a good mood.

What is different to a 'usual' day? Let's think back and list the differences.

Usual Day	Miraculous Day
Mum in a bad mood	Mum in a good mood
cereal for breakfast	fry up for breakfast
Bus to school	I have a new motorbike
Don't see my mates	My mates all at school
teacher irritated	Teacher friendly
Lessons in the afternoon	P.E all afternoon
hassle at home about T.V.	No hassle at home

Group Weekly Review Sheet.

Name of student	TARGET	Do we think it was achieved? YES	NO	Award points out of 10 for effort.
Janis	Not to shout out in Geography	✓		$\frac{8}{10}$
Chris	To remain in seat in French for at least 15 mins.		✗	$\frac{5}{10}$
Jason	To arrive at Maths. lesson in first 5 mins.	✓		$\frac{7}{10}$
Simon	To leave bad attitude at the door in French.		✓	$\frac{3}{10}$

CONCEPT 4
Being Cool in School

Key concept

For the majority of students, and invariably those who may be included in this programme, peer pressure forms a powerful and significant part of their daily experience. Looking cool or being considered cool in school will be an essential objective for most students. From the outset the facilitator will need to challenge quite explicitly the notion that it's all right or quite cool to be excluded. If students have had a number of fixed-term exclusions, it's no longer, a shock to be told to stay at home for a day – it's just part of what you do. For some students, choosing to get excluded becomes part of their self-defence mechanism. If they are going to continue to get excluded, then it is necessary for them to adopt the attitude that this doesn't really matter.

It is essential for the facilitator to be able to shift this perception and encourage the students to adopt a different set of beliefs and values, i.e. that it is cool to be in school and that they can survive in school. Central to this process is the fact that most students do survive in school, and that they don't actually behave like perfect little angels in this context. In order to successfully survive school you don't have to be a 'boffin', a 'goody goody' or a 'keener'. You can survive by being yourself, but you need to develop the right kind of survival skills in order to do so successfully. This is the central objective of this course – to enable the students to develop and make use of these skills in order to achieve the best possible outcome for themselves, and so remain 'cool' in school.

Consequently, we feel that this concept really needs to be addressed at the early stages of any planned intervention (and continually reinforced throughout the sessions). The question needs to be posed: 'What does it mean to get kicked out of school?' The students need to be able to identify and articulate both the positive and negative aspects and to be made aware of the negative chain reaction of events and consequences that this experience results in.

The students need to believe and accept that getting kicked out of school is, in fact, an entirely negative experience and totally 'uncool'.

Once this fact has been acknowledged and accepted, the students will need to develop an understanding of how they can continue to look good with their peers, whilst simultaneously reducing the behaviours that would get them into trouble. From the outset, this requires an extremely careful, but direct, approach. This issue is crucial for the students and needs to be addressed at the outset and discussed explicitly and openly with them. They will need to see and understand that there is a careful balance to be achieved, and that they need to develop the skills to achieve and maintain that balance. They need to develop ways to avoid the behaviours that they currently feel make them appear 'cool' in the eyes of their peers, but which frequently result in negative consequences for them. Part of this involves predicting and avoiding these 'problem' situations and continually thinking ahead to the consequences. The students may feel 'cool' when acting up in front of his/her peer group or confronting a teacher in front of the same audience - but how cool will they feel once they've been excluded and that audience has been taken away?

Who's cooler? The person enjoying the entertainment and leaving school with exams, or the clown who gets kicked out with no exams?

It is important to realise that however negative or destructive the behaviour may be, it is serving a purpose for the student – it is needs-driven. Even if the behaviour stops, the need behind the purpose will remain. Stripping away all the 'cool' behaviours which have caused problems in the past, but which have given the attention or approval of peers, would probably simply leave the student feeling naked in the school context. This would set them up for failure – no one can lose so much face in one go and still successfully survive. Students need to develop replacement behaviours that fill the gap in relation to peers but which will not get them into trouble. The targets need to be small and achievable. When we take away one 'cool' but destructive behaviour, we need to give the student something to replace it, i.e. the skills to avoid the confrontations or other negative patterns of behaviours being exhibited in front of their peers.

Illustrative script
Who is the coolest?

Teacher: Okay. I've got two scenarios for you to consider here. Both of them involve a kid having a confrontation with the teacher, but that's where the similarity ends, as one gets into further trouble and the other one manages to get himself out of it, before the situation gets too hot for him. They're on these two cards. Have a read:

Scene 1: who is the coolest?
Hannah goes into the classroom. She's in a bad mood as she's just had an argument with her mum in the car. Her mum said she'd have to stop her going out if she didn't start doing more coursework. Mr James (head of year) had phoned her to complain and also said that Hannah was showing a lot of attitude lately and being very lippy to members of staff. Hannah felt really fed up. She took out her nail file and started to do her nails just as Miss Simpson started the French lesson. Her friends started giggling - no one else would dare to be so visibly rude apart from Hannah. She was really cool. Miss Simpson said: "What are you doing?" Hannah said: "What does it look like?" Miss Simpson said: "There's no need to be rude Hannah". Hannah responded "Moi? But of course not. It's you that's rude. Just leave me alone to get on with it. Cow!" Miss Simpson said she'd had enough and told her to get out of the room. Hannah laughed, picked up her stuff and walked out.

Scene 2: who is the coolest?
Hannah goes into the classroom. She's in a bad mood as she's just had an argument with her mum in the car. Her mum said she'd have to stop her going out if she didn't start doing more coursework. Mr James (head of year) had phoned her to complain and also said that Hannah was showing a lot of attitude lately and being very lippy to members of staff. Hannah felt really fed up. She took out her nail file and started to do her nails just as Miss Simpson started the French lesson. Her

friends started giggling - no one else would dare to be so visibly rude apart from Hannah. She was really cool. Miss Simpson said: "What are you doing?". Hannah smiled and continued to file her left thumbnail. "Oh Miss - but I just don't have enough time. Honestly. I must concentrate on the really important things!" said Hannah, smiling as she put the file away.

Teacher:	Okay. Let's think about it. Who did you think was the coolest?
Ben:	I suppose it wasn't the first one - I mean she was funny and made her mates laugh.
Sara:	Yeah. But she took it too far. There's showing off and there's showing off. Once she'd been asked she should have just laughed - calling the teacher a cow wasn't cool.
Ben:	Yeah - she should have stopped before that. She could have saved face if she'd just laughed at the teacher and then put the file away. Her mates would still have thought she was funny.
Mel:	I think she just looked out of control and that's not cool - like she had so much anger in her that she was taking it out on the teacher. It's stupid to do that.
Teacher:	What about the second scene Ben - why do you think she was cooler?
Ben:	Well - it was the words she used. She wasn't trying to be confrontational and attack the teacher. She was just sort of teasing the teacher a bit.
Mel:	Yes. The teacher might even have smiled when Hannah was a bit rude - but the way that she said it wasn't that bad or nasty.
Sara:	She didn't look stupid in front of her mates, but she'd still made a point.
Mel:	That is cool - to get what you want without losing it.

Teaching the concept

Discussion and roleplay – what would you do?
Using group discussions to problem solve a range of situations, which may be perceived as attacks upon the student's self-esteem, is extremely useful. This is particularly so given that the facilitator will not be saying this is the right way to respond. Rather, they will be continually posing the question: what would you do?

- What would you do if the teacher shouted at you?
- What would you do if the teacher showed you up in front of your friends?
- What would you do if the teacher laughed at your answer?
- What would you do if the teacher wrongly accused you?
- What would you do if the teacher ignored you?
- What would you do if the teacher didn't listen to you?

The students need to be encouraged to formulate their own situations and not have them prescribed for them by the adults supporting them. It only works for you if you really own it! They need to identify, articulate and further develop a range of strategies and techniques that will allow them to remain 'cool' in a variety of conflict/problem situations.

Again, role-playing is an extremely useful tool here. It's no use simply talking around the problem. Students need to be given the opportunity to actually rehearse these skills. For example, the teacher is shouting at you. Show me how you respond. What are you doing to save face/keep cool/not lose it/remain in control?

Role-play is not something that everybody feels comfortable with. Indeed, with a student who has low self-esteem, lack of confidence, or who feels unsafe surrounded by their peers, this can be extremely threatening. It will be important for the facilitator to model how to role-play. This may mean the facilitator taking the role of the difficult student. Students are often more willing to take the role of the teacher (and can often be extremely punitive!). The modelling of the roles often involves self and peer parody, which can add to the enjoyment of roleplay, and eventually relaxation through participation in, roleplay.

At times, it may be necessary for the facilitator to play all the roles, encouraging participation by stopping the performance and then asking: "What do think they would have done next? What would they say next? Could you show me?".

<u>Working around peer pressure</u>
When talking with students, they will often not acknowledge the peer pressure that they will inevitably be experiencing. A stock response is 'I don't care what other people think', which can invariably be translated as the exact opposite in reality. It is important to encourage students to move on from this view and begin to acknowledge the everyday reality of peer pressure and the effects it has upon their feeling, beliefs and choices that they make about behaviour.

One way of approaching this tricky area is to highlight to students how even those that are 'strong' can be affected by peer pressure and yet still make the right choices in terms of ensuring the best outcome for themselves.

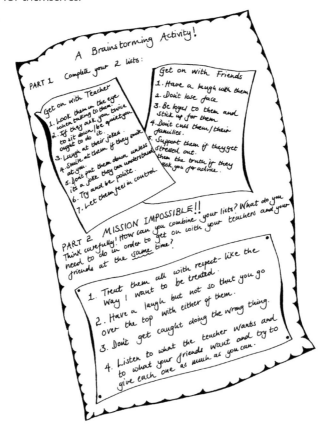

Initially, this topic is probably best covered by discussing how others respond to peer pressure using the third person. Some areas that may be useful in terms of promoting discussion are as follows:

- Nazi Germany
- Football crowds
- Teenage smoking and drinking
- Having sex
- Designer clothing
- Regional accents and street language

P.S.

- Students can explore what other people think about school and exclusion from school. It is possible to write letters to their heroes (footballers, singers etc.) asking for their views around this topic. Hopefully a helpful response will be forthcoming

- Students can draw up a pros and cons table in terms of exclusion. Part of this can cover the practicalities of what exclusion will mean, i.e. no exams, but boredom at home. Another part should encourage the students to explore what this will mean for them emotionally in terms of their own self-identity and vision of themselves

EXCLUSION BRAINSTORM.

Consequence	PRO's	CON's
You can meet up with other people	You have a great time	There may be nothing to do and you may have no money. Your friends might not be excluded as well.
you don't have any lessons	No teachers on your back No homework No boring lessons.	you don't learn anything You don't get better at your work. you feel stupid and don't pass any exams.

Think about it!!
• Which is more attractive to you in the short term? Why?
• Which is more attractive to you in the long term? Why?

CONCEPT 5
It's Not Fair

Key concept

Unfairness in society generates a tremendous amount of anger and resentment amongst the population in general. For young people who have a very low self-esteem and a poor self-image, and who may be treated unfairly on a fairly regular basis, the concept of fairness is magnified and plays a huge part in maintaining their feelings of disenfranchisement and powerlessness. These feelings very often block any movement towards a more positive situation and can mitigate against the changes that are needed to ensure a better outcome. For example, student responses to their poor behaviour will often highlight fairness as a reason why it's not **their** behaviour that needs to change, i.e. "It wasn't me! I didn't do anything. It was the teacher who was unfair".

Conflicting perceptions of events can often lead to problems remaining unresolved. Usually, this will involve the notion of 'fairness' and the pupil feeling that the situation is or was unfair. This state of stagnation must be totally bypassed. Teachers have tended to spend inordinate amounts of time posing as Sherlock Holmes style detectives in order to unpick specific problems and to find out 'why' the student feels that the teacher treated them unfairly or, very often, if this was actually the case at all. Sometimes, the student's perspective has not always been entirely accurate – possibly because he/she had not been able to really understand what was going on at the time – why the situation escalated, why the teacher may have been offended, or maybe he simply chose not to understand!

The following script shows an illustration of this:

Teacher: What do you mean, it's not fair?

Jason: It's not fair. I didn't do it. It wasn't my fault, yet I get the blame and get another detention. Well I'm not going to do it.

Teacher: So what did happen then?

Jason:	I came into class and Miriam tried to trip me over. I missed her foot and tripped over the chair leg. The chair slid across the floor and hit Mike on the ankle. He turned round and swore at me and went to throw the chair back at me. Miss shouted at him to put the chair down and she said that she had seen me kick the chair across at Mike and that it was my fault for starting it. I then argued with her saying it wasn't my fault. She said that it was always my fault and that I always caused trouble. She said that she had seen me kick the chair and that she would be talking to my head of year and I would have a detention. Then I stormed out of the room.
Teacher:	Well I'm not sure that that was a good idea to leave the room. It may have made her more angry.
Jason:	I don't care. She wasn't listening to me and she accused me of something that I didn't do. You ask Ben. He saw I didn't kick the chair. Shakiva and Gemma were there as well. Ask them.
Teacher:	OK. What lesson are you suppose to be in now? I better talk to them!

After this conversation, it is likely that the teacher will end up interviewing at least three other students and the classteacher. The stories presented are likely to be conflicting – reflecting pupil politics rather than an accurate picture of what went on. The original behaviour is unlikely to ever get addressed. There is very little likelihood of setting up a better situation for next time.

In order to get to a situation in which we can talk about behaviour, we need to get past this state of stagnation or the 'it's not fair' syndrome. The way in which it is proposed that this is done is by banning the words 'it's not fair'. Further to this, the facilitator can train the student to react to a 'known' set script in order to bypass these words.

The following statements could be used regularly with students. The frequency of use and the explicit discussion about their origins should mean that the students know the wording, as well as the facilitator who may be saying them!

"Do I care about how fair it was?"

"Do I care about fairness?"

"All I care about is what actually happened and what
the outcome was."

"I care about what you were doing, and what you will do next time."

It is important to have covered the origins of these statements before
using them. The student needs to understand that the concept of
fairness may get in the way of them solving the difficulty or problem
and getting the best outcome for themselves.

Many of the situations that the students are placed in aren't fair and
this is why the skills and strategies covered throughout these sessions
aim to support and keep them in getting the best outcome for
themselves from a range of situations which aren't particularly good.
The imagery of 'surviving school' and battling through against the
odds is evident here, and it is something that many of the students
positively respond to. It can be acknowledged that there are a lot of
things that are unfair, but what we want for the students is that they
can get the best possible deal out of even the most unfair situations.
Dwelling on whether or not it's fair is basically a fruitless exercise, but
formulating solutions and making the best of a tricky situation is far
more positive and productive. Again, this is a solution-focused process
– looking forwards towards a better outcome rather than dwelling
endlessly and fruitlessly upon any 'unfairness'. However, we do
acknowledge the fact that some teachers find this concept a tricky
one to handle and take on board. The question continually 'posed' is:
'why should the pupils have to put up with unfairness?' It is important
to highlight that other issues need to be simultaneously addressed, i.e.
the whole school behaviour management structure and the way that
students are treated and spoken to by the staff in the school.

This, however, is *School Survival,* and for the majority of students
undertaking this course, this is the end of the road – a last chance to
change and cope effectively in school. These are the students who
don't have time for the systems to change or for the teachers to 'get
better'. What they need to be encouraged to do is to be able to
describe and acknowledge the 'unfair' situation, and then get
themselves out of it – gaining the best possible outcome at that

moment in time. This is the moment at which the facilitator/teacher can turn round to the student and say "Hey – that wasn't really fair – but you managed to get yourself out of it. How did you do that?" This is a very empowering reversal.

Illustrative script
The 'it's not fair' script

Pupil: But it isn't fair - why should I get chucked out of class just because the teacher's in a bad mood and wants to take it out on me?

Teacher: But I'm not interested in fairness or 'how fair' it was.

Pupil: Yeah - but it just isn't fair.

Teacher: Do I care about fairness?

Pupil: No - I know you don't.

Teacher: Right, so just tell me what actually happened. Can you go back and describe it?

Pupil: Yeah - I was having an argument with Ben when we were going into class. He kept on saying that Eric and me were thickos because we'd been put into the bottom set for Maths. I told him he was a gay twit and Mr Roberts overheard me. He said that I should refrain from my homophobia and get myself into a seat straightaway. I said to him that it was up to me if I didn't like poofs and he shouted "get out - you don't deserve to be here". I thought that was unfair - like he was picking on me. So I told him to f... off big-time.

Teacher: What would I have seen?

Pupil: Well - like this [pupil acts over the top behaviour].

Teacher: Do you think that was cool?

Pupil: Well - my mates laughed, but I knew it was one step too far.

Teacher: Well - that's important. There's one positive outcome for you. You could actually recognise that boundary.

Pupil: But it still wasn't fair, because Ben didn't get told off for saying I was thick.

Teacher: It's not the fairness here - it's what you did. I think the best thing is for us to think through it all again and work out what would have got you a better outcome. What do you think?

Pupil:	Okay.
Teacher:	How could you have responded?
Pupil:	If I had told him to shut up or just ignored it, it would probably have been cooler - but it's hard because if I didn't say anything then I would look stupid in front of all the other kids. You can't let someone cuss you like that and get away with it. It makes you look wet and soft.
Teacher:	So what about saying something quite strong back, but keeping calm when you do it. What do you think about that?
Pupil:	Like what? I don't know the words.
Teacher:	Well, like - why is someone so intelligent being so nasty? Why does he need to put other people down?
Pupil:	Mmm - okay. I would say " Just shut it you (I'd miss out the gay bit) and leave me alone. If you're so clever, why do you need to show yourself up by being so big-headed and trying to put me down. You're just a prat". If I said that, then at least I wouldn't get in so much trouble.
Teacher:	Yes - it might not get you such a negative outcome!

Teaching the concept

<u>Assertiveness</u>
It is often useful to teach the students what it is to be assertive – how to get their needs met without being aggressive or causing trouble to themselves or others. A useful teaching method is to play the game 'What would you say to people?'.

Roleplay or discuss the following situations:
- 'You smell' – how do you tell someone they have body odour (nicely)
- 'I don't want to do drugs' – how can you say no without being condemnatory to you friends?
- 'It wasn't me!' – someone accuses you of something you haven't done. What do you say without getting into more trouble then, or in the future?

- 'Could you turn the music down?' – you are trying to go to sleep and the next door neighbour is playing their music very loudly. How can you sort this one out?
- 'Don't say that about my Mum!' – someone is trying to wind you up and is being rude about your mum. What do you say?

It is useful to explain the distinction between assertive, being aggressive and being passive. It may be useful to encourage the students to act out responses to the situations listed above and to those situations that they meet in everyday life.

Life is unfair

It may be useful to explore a wider debate with students and to discuss things in society which represent models of unfairness. Such issues can range from someone being taller and so being able to see at a concert, through to issues of racism and disability discrimination.

Developing strategies for tackling unfairness in the classroom

Using real life events and instances is often a useful tool for getting students to construct alternative ways of responding to situations that they perceive to be unfair. This solution-focused strategy encourages them to identify, practice and ultimately replace negative response such as shouting, hitting and answering back, with more positive assertive response, ultimately ensuring a better outcome.

Roleplay

Students can be encouraged to respond to Mr Un Fair in a way that doesn't get them into trouble. The facilitator (or pupil) takes on the role of Mr Un Fair and in a one to one roleplay situation aims to provoke the student to react in a negative way by being unfair – by picking on them or being critical. The remaining group members act as observers and are required to assess when the student has gone too far, i.e. when they actually become aggressive or rude to Mr Un Fair.

Problem page

Students can be asked to formulate solutions to a range of 'unfair' problem page letters.

Dear Sue,
    I've got a problem with this one teacher who just doesn't like me. She always picks on me and gives me detentions when I haven't done anything. I get accused of doing stuff I haven't done all the time. What should I do?
    yours, Darren.

P.S.

- It can often be useful to watch films such as *Cry Freedom* and *Ghandi* in order to set unfairness in a whole world context. The students are not the only ones in the world that are exposed to unfairness

- Discussions with the students can focus on how anger is generated when people perceive things as unfair. Getting the students to explore their emotional response when they feel something is unfair is often a useful way forward

- Look at 'fair' from other perspectives. Do teachers think it is fair that they misbehave? Is it fair that the other students in their class get their learning interrupted because of the constant disruption in the class caused by those who misbehave?

CONCEPT 6
Power to The Pupil

Key concept

This concept centres on the empowerment of the students. The facilitator's role here is to highlight how each student has the power to affect change in themselves and in their situations. It is when the student feels disempowered that he will abdicate responsibility for his behaviour, and for the outcomes and consequences of that behaviour. Again, we are also reinforcing the idea that this is your behaviour and you own it. However, giving power back to the students in this way is not, by any means, a simple or easy task – particularly when those students will have developed a range of negative patterns of behaviour and experienced a great deal of negative feedback which is damaging to their self-esteem and confidence. Initially, it is important to stress that they are not expected to change on their own, and that you, the facilitator, are there to help and support them in regaining their power.

One way of going about this sensitive task is to initially focus upon the fact that it is possible to survive class – most people genuinely do survive it – on a daily basis. When looking at statistics this becomes very evident, and it is important to show the students this kind of evidence and allow them to compare the small number of pupils who are permanently excluded with the number who remain, apparently quite successfully, within the mainstream context. Students need to understand that developing and maintaining the 'power' to keep out of trouble and survive school, is not the enormous goal or set of miraculous skills that they may think it is. Staying out of trouble doesn't have to be seen as a 'big deal'.

Illustrative script
Locus of control

Teacher: Okay - lets have a look at the locus of control cards. These are the statements I'd like you to consider. Here's the first one: "I kicked the ball really well and scored a goal". What do you think - is that the internal or external control?

Ted:	Internal - because he kicked it and scored and he wasn't relying on anyone else or blaming anyone else.
Teacher:	The second one is this: "I did well in the spelling test because I revised".
Jane:	Internal again. Because I revised - I did it myself. No one else did it for me.
Teacher:	Okay - the third one is this: "I was good in class so I got two points".
Ted:	It's internal again because I did it - it was my behaviour and I owned it.
Teacher:	Okay - how about this one: "The goal keeper dived the wrong way and I kicked the ball and scored".
Ted:	That's easy. It's external. Because he's saying that he only scored because the goalkeeper dived the wrong way. He's blaming it on the goalkeeper being rubbish.
Teacher:	Great. That's it. How about this one: "The test was easy so I did well on it".
Jane:	That's external because it's like - she didn't do it on her own. She only did well because the test was easy. She's blaming the outcome on the test (even though it was a good one for her). It's like she's saying she couldn't have done well if it was harder. She's not taking the right sort of credit.
Teacher:	Okay - what about this one: "The teacher was in a bad mood so I lost two behaviour points". What's that, internal or external control?
Ted:	External. Because he's blaming the teacher for the outcome when it was his behaviour that did it. That's what lost him the two points. It's down to him. He's not accepting responsibility for the outcome.
Teacher:	Great. You've both got it. You're giving me really brilliant answers here. Now, let's just set them out into two columns. We'll put the external control sentences in one column and the internal control sentences in another. What do you notice when you read them?

Ted:	Well, the internal control situations all start with I, I, I...
Jane:	...and the external control ones start with <u>the</u> - the goalkeeper, the test, the teacher...
Teacher:	That's it. So what we want to get to is a place where 'I' is in control and accepting responsibility for the outcomes...okay?
Ted & Jane:	Okay Miss!

Teaching the concept

<u>The keeping quiet strategy</u>

One way of reinforcing the notion that staying out of trouble doesn't have to be seen as a big deal or an impossible task, is to ask the student: "If you were quiet and didn't say anything for the whole of the lesson, would you get into trouble?" Initially, many of the students will respond that they would get into trouble, and will genuinely believe this to be a fact. They need to move on from such a position and begin to envisage a better and more positive outcome from such a strategy, and having the opportunity to try it out and review it is essential.

<u>The snake charmer</u>

Introducing the idea of the snake charmer, who treats his dangerous snakes with kindness and respect so that he can get very close to them without getting bitten, is another good visual image to use when returning power to the pupil. The snake handler reads the body language, mood and movements of the snake, gaining information so that he can behave in a way that will not aggravate the snake.

The students can be asked to imagine their teachers in the role of the snake! If they treat the teachers well and respond kindly and wisely to any specific characteristics or behaviours, then they are more likely to successfully survive the lesson. After all, the snake doesn't actually want to bite, as it loses energy and venom when it has to attack in this way.

Seeing it from the teacher's viewpoint

Students can be asked to describe a teacher's day from the moment that they get up in the morning to the moment when they go back to bed. They can consider the feelings that the teacher may have and describe the behaviour that they exhibit in each lesson, noting if these change at all and why, i.e. for different year groups/classes. What happens at lunch and break times? What do the students think the teachers do and say at these times? Alternatively, it would be useful to ask a teacher in the school to provide a description of his/her day (in confidence of course!), which would actually show the students just what an ordinary, tiring and often mundane job this is (along with a few flashes of inspiration). What is important is that the students are able to take on board the fact that teachers do not sit around, either at home or at school, devising and plotting ways to upset, humiliate and exclude their students.

A further strategy to develop the student's empathy and understanding of the teacher's position is to ask them to interview members of staff and specifically ask them about what it's like to have to cope with negative behaviours from students. They can work on the questionnaires prior to the interviews so that they have a consistent framework to work through. Questions might include:

- What do you think 'bad' behaviour is?
- When does it tend to happen?
- Why do you think students do these things?
- How do they feel?
- What do you do to try and stop them?
- How do you help them?
- How does their behaviour make you feel?
- Do you like being a teacher?

Locus of control

It is probably essential that at least one or a significant part of one session focuses upon this concept. The students need to be taught the distinction between external and internal control. Explain that if you blame others or the context for your behaviour, then the control is external, whereas if you accept responsibility for what you do and the choices that you make, then you have internal control. All the students need to be aware of the need to develop and maintain this internal control – as this is what provides them with their power. Accepting a portion of external control will simply dis-empower the student once again.

Eventually this should allow the pupil to analyse any situation, identifying where the locus of control may fall. It is important to ensure that the students learn to not internalise control over things that they have no power to control (for example – which teacher they get for geography). However, it is important to help the students identify things that they can and should take control over (for example – the relationship that you have with the geography teacher).

In terms of *School Survival* and survival skills in general, it might also be useful to discuss how the explorer doesn't have any control over the weather, and is therefore better externalising that locus. But he has an internal locus of control over how he will survive any adverse weather conditions.

Providing the students with a variety of scripts or example words is a useful strategy. They can distinguish between those characters who have an internal locus of control and those that have an external locus of control. For example: "I did well in the maths test because I worked hard and revised a lot" shows an internal locus of control as the student is taking responsibility for revising and for the outcome of that revision – it was down to me. "I did well on the test because it was easy" shows an external locus of control. The student is saying that he/she had no control over the test and his/her input was irrelevant – it was down to the test being easy!

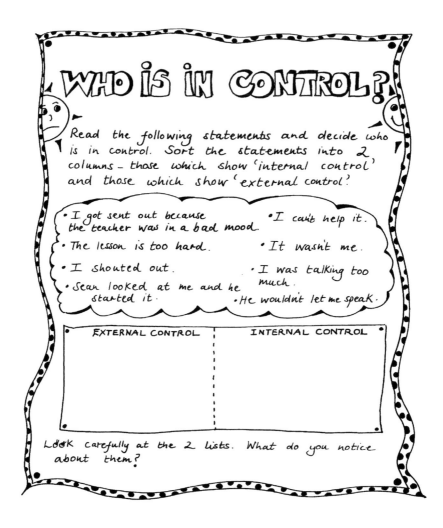

The students can then be encouraged to make up their own scripts. This is a very powerful tool as the students can actually hear themselves using this internal control and abdicating responsibility when the script details external control. For example, when the student says "but the teacher was being horrible", they will be able to reflect more upon this statement and quickly identify it as being a statement of external control. Developing these thought processes and 'scripts' can clearly impact upon the classroom and be transferred from the group into the larger context.

P.S.

- Use real statistics from your school or education authority to show the small percentage of students who don't make it in school compared with the large number who do. It is probably best not to use percentages, but use actual pupil numbers

- The students can do a case study of a student who survives lessons. In this case study, they could draw out the key elements that help that individual survive

- It is sometimes useful to ask a teacher or headteacher to give a talk for 10 minutes about 'My day'

Case Study
of a student who does survive
lessons.

Name:
D.O.B.:
Yr. Group:

1. What did he/she do? Were they good all the time?

2. How did the teacher react?

3. What helped them to survive?

4. Which 2 things would you say you could do?

Example PROBLEM CARD

I get angry when

I arrive late for lessons and the teacher shouts at me

and doesn't give me a chance to speak.

Think! How do you currently deal with this?

I shout back and kick my chair or sometimes I walk out

of the lesson.

How could you deal with this more positively?

Not shout back

Sit down quietly

Apologise for being late

Act out the situation and devise both a positive and negative way of dealing with it.

CONCEPT 7
Don't Tell Me – Show Me!

Key concept

Students targeted through the *School Survival* course may often have a wealth of experience of being talked 'to' or 'at' by teachers, their head of year, or members of the school's pastoral team, and they will consequently have developed the ability to 'talk the talk'. They will be able to listen and respond to the 'you know what you should be doing' approach, having heard it from adults both in and out of the school context. But, like a tape recorder or record that continuously gets stuck and repeats each section, these words will have little impact on them and will certainly not touch them internally. What they will be able to do in response to this, is use the same 'talk' and convince the adults that they have listened and taken on board their 'advice'.

The 'don't tell me – show me' concept is a reaction against such time wasting and meaningless talk. This approach asks the students to show that they have understood the concepts being covered by showing the facilitator positive behaviours and outcomes, i.e. I will know that you've understood this and that your behaviour is right if you show me; I will know that you understand these concepts because you'll be showing me that you do; you won't be telling me what you should be doing but you will be showing me. In order to cut through and limit any previously developed talents in 'talking the talk', the facilitator will be continually restating the same request: I don't want you to tell me what you should be doing; I want you to show me. As with the other skills and strategies discussed, the only way of measuring any success is by defining the extent to which they have been transferred into the classroom. Unless the students can 'show' that they've understood the concepts by modifying their behaviours, beliefs and attitudes within the classroom context, then the intervention will have failed. There is absolutely no point in the students being able to accurately describe their behaviour and have articulate discussions about the locus of control, if they can't actually use these concepts, skills and ideas in real life.

The central emphasis throughout the course must be on maximising the student's ability to change their behaviour in the classroom.

The 'don't tell me – show me' script, much like 'do I care if it's not fair?' will be made use of throughout the sessions. It will hopefully become part of the survival kit that the students carry around with them and make use of in order to cope effectively in a range of situations. Hopefully, these types of scripts will act as triggers, with the student being able to complete the prompts from the facilitator:
Teacher: Don't tell me
Student: Show me!

Via the use of objective, descriptive language, and by reflecting and analysing their behaviours, the students should be able to identify the specific situations that would trigger the use of such scripts. This should also have a knock-on effect for their behaviour.

Using the group to reinforce and encourage use of such scripts is vital. Once the scripts have been introduced, explained and used within the group context, the students can support each other in transferring them to the classroom.

The aim is to enable the students to make the journey from a conditioned response to one in which they are able to reflect upon their behaviour, subsequently make a positive choice, and then act appropriately.

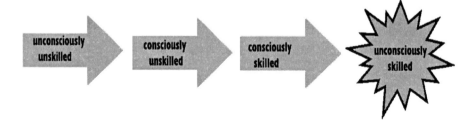

In order to explain this process to the students, the facilitator can make use of an army drill analogy.

- Soldiers can strip a gun down under any type of pressure and in any circumstances. This is an unconscious act that is carried out without thought or planning – it becomes instinctive
- The students need to be able to develop their own skills in terms of acting in an automatic way in a range of situations. Initially these skills are going to be taught and learnt within the group context. There must be copious opportunities for students to develop automatic, 'positive' responses to a range of conflict situations. For example, when the teacher is shouting at you for being late, when you can't do the work, when you've had an argument with your mum, when someone has given you a dirty look, etc
- The facilitator needs to help the students identify the possible situations that could cause problems. Taking these real life situations, it is then possible to roleplay the confrontation, constructing and practising a rigid response. The central idea is to become so skilled at giving the right response that they are able to do this even under pressure and provocation

As with the model of the soldier under pressure – when they are able to do things automatically that will keep them alive (or in the classroom), it is then that they can use their thoughts to make calmer choices about how to overcome and survive the situation even better.

Illustrative script

Teacher:	Okay Michael. Just tell me again. What would you do if the teacher had accused you of doing something in the lesson, like shouting out/being rude, but you know that it definitely wasn't you?. How would you handle that in order to get a best possible outcome for yourself?
Michael:	Well I think I would just say to that teacher "It really wasn't me. Honest" and if they went on, I'd just sit down and be quiet. It would be no good getting back at them, as it would just get worse.

Teacher: What else might you do?

Michael: I'd try and really keep my mouth shut and keep really quiet - just getting on with my work. That way it would look as if I was a bit sorry and wanted to make it up - even though I wouldn't be sorry. I'd hold onto it until the end of the lesson. Then I'd go up to the teacher and say again that it wasn't me but I'd say it quietly and look at them, so that they didn't think I was being rude. I'd say it like I meant it. If she gave me a detention I'd just have to go with it - even though it's not fair. I'd make sure I just sat on my own next time, which might work better.

Teacher: Okay. You've 'told it' brilliantly. I like the idea of the quiet sorry when you are looking at them. It would probably get you a better outcome. Now what did actually happen?

Michael: I blew it. I shouted that it wasn't me that got her feeling angry, as she was worried about the kids thinking she was losing it. I was mad at her for picking on me again and making me feel like I was a prat in front of my mates. I got chucked out.

Teacher: So you can 'tell' me what you should have done...why was it so difficult to do it? What stopped you?

Michael: I think it was how I felt.

Teacher: Yes?

Michael: Well - angry and stupid. Shown up again. It made me have that kind of humiliated, hot feeling - like my face was red and I could feel my heartbeat getting faster and faster.

Teacher: I can see that it's much harder. It's the same for everyone when that sense of panic sets in - but how are you going to get round this? What do you think you could do to help yourself out here and 'show' the other kind of behaviour?

Michael: I've got to get over being shown up and not mind - I've got to try and answer her with a quiet voice and keep it respectful. If I can sort of stop myself and think before I open my mouth, it might help. I suppose I could just try and think 'show me - don't tell me' or something, over and over in my head so I don't lose it.

Teacher: Okay. So let's make that the target for next week - not to get chucked out of that lesson. Use the script and show me that you can do this by this time next week. Okay?

Michael: Okay!

Teaching the concept

Roleplay/video

Asking the students to develop their own scripts which they can use at point of conflict/choice points during lessons will be extremely useful, as will subsequently 'acting out' these scripts. Students can formulate two scenes – one in which they don't make use of their script at the point of conflict, and one in which they do. The latter scene will clearly illustrate the better outcome/the best possible outcome. Videoing the scenes will then allow the students to further analyse and reflect upon their behaviours and to pose solution-focused questions such as: What would be an even better outcome? How could I achieve that? What could I do differently? How could I help myself even more? How could I control my anger?

Script diaries

Students can keep a weekly diary – recording the times when they used their scripts in order to effect a change in behaviour in class. This will also allow further analysis and reflection and aid the target setting process. Students will be able to highlight the most significant difficulties and then really target these during the coming week. As each student will be aware of everyone else's targets, there should also be opportunities to support each other in using their scripts. This support/ intervention could also be recorded in the diaries.

P.S.

- It is often useful to look at action heroes (such as Lara Croft, Indiana Jones and James Bond) on videos and films. The focus here should be how the film portrays them as cool and calm in very stressful situations. They cannot allow their thoughts to be over run by emotions, which would then swamp their ability to make good choices. It is obviously useful to point out that these are only film characters, and that it is much more difficult in real life! But the principle is much the same.

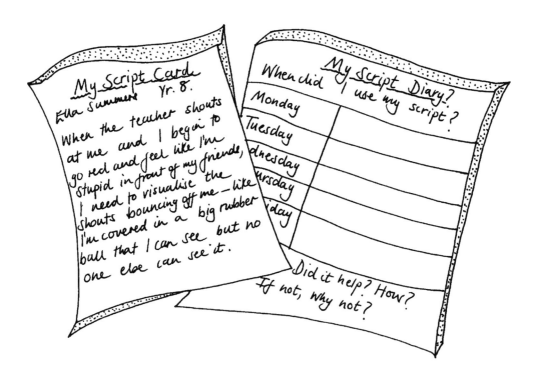

CONCEPT 8
It's for Real – Getting the Talk Into the Classroom

Key concept

This concept is linked to the previous concept: Don't Tell Me – Show Me. The idea here is to ensure that the good work done in the group is transferred into the classroom – the positive conversations, the skills and strategies, the different beliefs, values and perceptions – all need to be evident in the behaviour of each group member within both contexts. The success of any group of this kind needs to be measured in this way and is crucial.

One key to ensuring such transference of skills and behaviours is to continually provide students with the opportunity to role play every situation, every verbal confrontation, every piece of body language and every skill taught. The expected behaviours need to be modelled at every point and students should be given opportunities to actually practice the behaviours that will ensure them the best possible outcome. The learning and rehearsing process is essential if, as discussed earlier, we can't rely on rational, non-emotive thought in the classroom. Whenever we are presenting ourselves (particularly in stressful situations such as interviews or performances of any kind) we need to practice and prepare. What are we going to say? What will we look like? How will we sit? Who will we look at? The students need to feel absolutely prepared and skilled in order to make the best choices and achieve the best outcomes. Surviving school will be a stressful experience for most of them, and we need to ensure that they feel confident in taking up this challenge. 'Practice makes perfect' may not be the most suitable phrase here, but could perhaps be translated into 'practice improves the likelihood of getting you the best possible outcome'.

It is very important to create the right context for this modelling and roleplay process. Much group work tends to take place in a circle, as this creates an ethos of sharing, support and co-operation.

There may well be moments in this course that such a context is entirely appropriate. However, for the purposes of learning new behaviours and observing and analysing old ones, it is recommended that the 'group room' be set out as a classroom with the desks in rows facing the front of the room. This may even represent an identified classroom in the school where there are acknowledged difficulties. If the students are going to be able to transfer their new knowledge and skills into the classroom context, then they need to be provided with an environment which is as near to the real thing as they are likely to get. This may well include not just the formal layout, but also the expectations of behaviour when initially coming into the group room, i.e. the students are expected to fully comply with the usual classroom rules and expectations, and come into the room in the 'standard' fashion. They may even be asked to line up outside – whatever is the normal school procedure. What matters is that they practice doing it 'right' in the 'nearly real' context – where they can be given support – so that they then have more chance of getting it 'right' in the 'really real' context.

This may require a more general focus on what the usual classroom expectations are. For example, if students are not allowed to chew, sit on desks, shout out or swear in the classroom context, then exactly the same rules will need to apply within the group, at all times. It is important to highlight the fact that if students are not given every chance to manage these behaviours in the smaller group context (hopefully with a highly skilled facilitator) then they will simply have no chance to do so in the classroom context. I.e. "If you can't show me here, then you certainly won't be able to show me there."

Obviously, the context does not have to be a classroom one throughout the entirety of any one session, or in all of the sessions. This set up is designed purely to enable the students to model and practice the required behaviours within the most naturalistic setting possible, to allow easier transference. There will be many occasions when a circle set up is entirely appropriate, and more conducive to learning and positive interaction, for example, when working on locus of control activities. However, as the students have more and more opportunities to practice and rehearse the 'appropriate' behaviours – hand up to answer, lining up sensibly, sitting forward, not shouting out, not chewing and so on – they will actually start to perceive themselves as individuals who can 'do' these behaviours. They will begin to see that it's not impossible to be able to put your hand up, come into the room quietly and sit appropriately at your desk. It is within their grasp and they do have the power within themselves to control their behaviour and to really get the ideas into the classroom. They can make this a reality for themselves.

Illustrative script

Teacher: Right, now today I'm going to take on the role of a student in class and I'd like you guys to sit up the front there - in a row behind the desk - and imagine that you are the teacher. I'm going to go out and then come back into the classroom. The first time I come in I'm going to do it with an attitude and the second time I'm going to do it in a way that I know will get me the best possible outcome from you - as the teacher. Okay?

Ben & Joseph: Okay

Teacher: While I'm acting the part I'll be asking you questions and asking you to describe my behaviour. Here goes.
[Teacher goes out and then pushes through the door and slumps down into the chair].

Teacher: Okay - what am I doing?

Ben: You're slumping - like you're tired and fed up and don't want to be there.

Joseph: You've put your legs on the table and you're leaning back and yawning and looking round the room.

Teacher: Okay - if you are the teacher, how do you feel now? What is my behaviour saying to you?

Ben: You're bored. You're not going to take any notice of what the teacher is going to say.

Teacher: What else?

Joseph: Your body is saying just don't bother tackling me, leave me alone - it's like you're asking for trouble. I'd be pretty mad by now if I was the teacher.

Ben: I'd be a bit angry, but I would ask you to sit properly - this is a lesson you know!

Teacher: What does my face say to that [yawns and raises her eyebrows]?

Ben: I don't care.

Joseph: I'd be even madder then - I'd chuck you out I think.

Ben: I would - but only if you swore and didn't sit up on the third chance.

Teacher: Okay - watch me again [goes out and then comes back into the room, quietly going to her seat, sitting down and taking out the necessary equipment for the start of the lesson]. What's different now?

Ben: You're OK.

Teacher: Yes, but what do you see?

Ben: You're sitting forward and quite still - you're not slumping on the desk and your feet are on the floor.

Joseph: You look as if you're going to work.

Teacher: How would that make you feel if you were the teacher?

Ben: Okay - I'd know I could leave you alone I suppose.

Joseph: I'd be glad - and I think I'd relax a bit and enjoy the lesson a bit more because I wouldn't be worried about having to tell you to stop - and then there wouldn't be a big scene - so, yeah, relieved really.

Teacher: What else can you tell from how I look?

Ben: You looked less angry than before - like you're in quite a good mood now - you're not tapping and looking around.

Joseph :   Or yawning...and the fact that you've got your pen out makes you look as if you're going to start work.

Teacher: Do you think that I'd get chucked out of class now?

Ben: No - because you're doing the right behaviours and the teacher won't have anything to complain about - as long as you don't start chatting to your mates.

Teacher: Right - now you can have a go. You know exactly what behaviours we want to see and you can do them. The more you practice, the more likely it is that you'll do them in the real classroom. What do you think?

Ben: Okay - I'll have a go.

Teacher: Great!

Teaching the concept

<u>Roleplay/video</u>
It is a good idea to have a range of 'problem behaviour' cards made up for roleplay sessions. These can detail a range of situations, e.g. coming into class, dealing with cursing, being told off for talking, being asked to do something you're not keen on. The students can then 'act out' and comment upon the responses to the negative behaviour, and the response which will achieve the best possible outcome. Once again, the video can be used to record the scenes and the students can then be encouraged to reflect and comment upon their work with a particular focus upon body language, tone of voice and the language used.

Problem Card

My friend keeps getting bullied because he's black. We're going to have to do something to stop it.

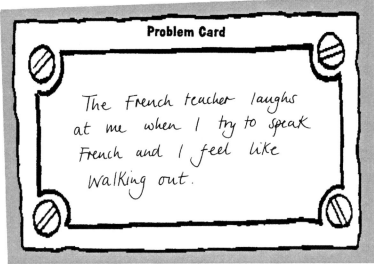

Problem Card

The French teacher laughs at me when I try to speak French and I feel like walking out.

'Real life' problems

If the students have had a problem during the previous week or day, then it is entirely appropriate to discuss it in the group context and model the behaviours that would have achieved a better result. Again, this is a further opportunity to problem solve and then practice the 'right' responses. What will you do in a similar situation next time? How will you look? What will you say? Show me the behaviours and let's get it back into the classroom! This can also be further developed as students can begin to identify patterns in their behaviour and attempt to pre-empt these from re-occurring 'next time'.

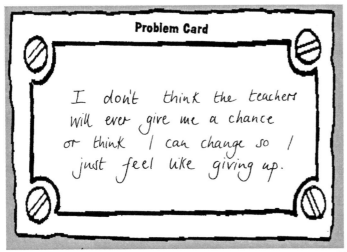

Problem Card

I don't think the teachers will ever give me a chance or think I can change so I just feel like giving up.

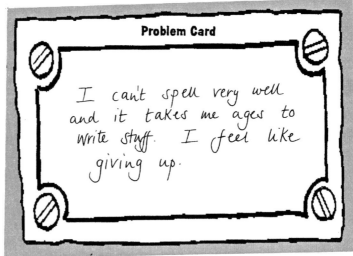

Problem Card

I can't spell very well and it takes me ages to write stuff. I feel like giving up.

Observing yourself / observing others

Students can monitor both their own behaviours and those of each other. They can devise a 'quick tick list' in order to record each occasion within a target session when they actually 'do' the 'right' behaviour. This device can, of course, be linked to part of the weekly target setting process, and can be used as a tool to reinforce and build each student's self-esteem and ability to empathise and support others.

Peer group descriptions

What is important when encouraging pupils to feedback on each other's behaviour or on a specific incident, is to ensure that they really do make accurate, objective descriptions – really developing their abilities to reflect upon and describe behaviour. If group members are describing the behaviour of one student in the group, it is helpful and supportive if the facilitator continually returns to this pupil for confirmation – is that right, is that how it was? Hearing how you did or didn't transfer your behaviour into the classroom from your peers is an extremely powerful strategy – not forgetting that this should be done as objectively and as non-judgementally as possible.

P.S.

- Sometimes it can be useful when discussing real life situations to develop group supportive strategies focused on one student's needs. In other words, encouraging the students to think about what it is that they could do to support their peer at times of stress. How might they themselves want support during these times? What were they doing when their friend got into trouble? And did this help or hinder them?

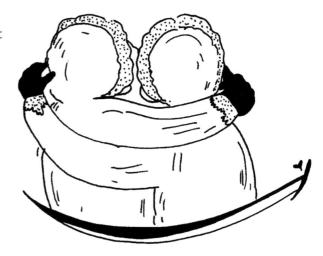

P.P.S. An important note

- When the students begin to describe 'real' situations, this will involve describing the behaviours and responses of members of staff involved in these confrontations/ interactions. It may become difficult to always avoid the fact that some of the ways in which the students are being treated is not alright. This is when the 'I don't care if it's not fair – am I interested in fairness?' script will need to dominate proceedings.

Useful scripts for this situation are:
- We all see things differently, don't we?
- What would the class teacher say about what happened?
- I wasn't there, tell me about what you did and what you had some control over?
- What would you do differently next time?

The facilitator must continually stress that they are not interested in what the teacher is doing. At no point can they be seen to support the student over the teacher. All the facilitator is doing is helping the students to develop their own skills in a variety of situations. The student does not have total control over each situation and the ways in which the teachers may or may not respond. They must focus only on what they do have control over. It is also a good idea to ensure that the school staff are made aware of this at the onset of the course. It's the student's behaviour that is being worked on here, not the teacher's behaviour management skills and strategies.

It is very important that the student feels that you are supportive, but you cannot be in the business of taking sides. One danger is the formation of a sub-culture. This is not healthy, especially when you are working to help the students survive in the mainstream environment. This is a central aim of the course – not to simply have access to a sub-culture with an ethos of "oh, it doesn't really matter – I know you're a good kid really." This is dangerous and unethical in our view. The purpose is to focus on changing student behaviour so that they have access to the mainstream culture and therefore remain included.

CONCEPT 9
Using the School Discipline
Structure as a Framework

Key concept

Again, this concept is directly linked to the previous concept, It's for real – getting the talk into the classroom, in that the discipline structure of the school needs to be an intrinsic part of this course throughout it's duration. The students will, at all times, be trained to actually work within that structure, and their targets will be set in order to help them remain and become further included within this framework. The course will not be setting up something 'extra' or 'different' to this structure, but will hopefully be providing them with the skills and resources to cope with it.

However, what does need to be addressed and carefully considered is the extent to which the school discipline policy or structure is consistently applied. Invariably, in our experience, lack of consistency has been an issue in most schools. There has been a tremendous amount of variation between teacher's perceptions and understanding of the policy and their application of it within the classroom context. The students will be trained to respond appropriately within such a structure, and may consequently have to suffer the humiliation of failure when the structure is suddenly changed. For example, they may have been told that they have access to three warnings prior to being kicked out of class, but then find themselves excluded at the first (and sometimes slightest) misdemeanour.

This is where, again, the 'do I care if it's not fair' script has come into play. Obviously, this may initially seem to be a rather harsh approach, but as detailed in the previous chapter, it is essential to maintain such a stance if we are to ensure that a sub-culture does not develop, and that no-one (namely the facilitator) is compromised. It is perhaps quite a bitter pill to swallow. But the alternative is harsher – being excluded – and consequently the focus needs to be entirely on developing the skills to read these situations more effectively. This is probably the hardest lesson to learn, accept and adopt – and not just for the students. The facilitator may also continually need to be prepared to swallow many of these bitter pills!

However, it is possible to address some of these difficulties if approached in a sensitive and thoughtful way. One important aspect of the facilitator's role can be to approach the teacher, who was involved in the conflict with the student, and sensitively and tactfully clarify exactly what the teacher's expectations were, and what they will be in future lessons. This will enable the facilitator to go back and set realistic and appropriate targets with the student, as well as stressing the importance of consistent practice to the teacher involved.

Illustrative script

Teacher: Okay. Let's look at the rule. What does it say? [Handing a copy of the school's discipline policy to Lara.]

Lara: It says that students will be provided with three opportunities to comply with a teacher's request and on failing to do so will be asked to leave the classroom and report to the head of year in order to complete a detention slip. Detention will take place...

Teacher: Right - that's fine. Do you think that's clear?

Lara: It might be clear but it's not what happens - that would be fair then. It would be the same for everybody.

Teacher: Hold on - remember - we're not talking about what's fair here. We're talking about you handling your behaviour in that class - no matter what happens - and doing the behaviours that don't get you chucked out.

Lara: Yeah, but she ignored that rule, so I didn't get the same chance.

Teacher: Fine - I can accept that, but we're not here to talk about her. She's not the issue here. The issue is about you and what you didn't do so that you got chucked out and didn't meet your target - okay?

Lara: I suppose so.

Teacher: We're not into 'suppose' - we're into facts - so just tell me the facts. Describe it to me.

Lara: I waited in the line outside the classroom and I stood at

	the front and I was just standing there. I was talking quietly to Michael - like we agreed. I wasn't being loud or shouting my mouth off.
Teacher:	Well, that's great. That is actually the behaviour you said you would do - so you definitely met that target. Then what?
Lara:	Miss came out and told us all to go in quietly. I walked to my desk and sat down. Michael handed me a piece of chewing gum under the table and I took it. I wasn't going to eat it but I was going to put it in my bag for break. Then Miss saw me putting it into the side pocket and she thought I was taking it out to eat it then and there in the lesson. She said "What is wrong with you? You've only been in this room for two minutes and already you are visibly breaking the rules. It's just typical of you - you just don't seem to understand what you're here for". I took a deep breath before I said anything because I didn't want to lose it.
Teacher:	Well that's even better - another target you've met.
Lara:	I didn't talk loudly. I put the gum in the side pocket of the bag and I said "I wasn't going to eat it Miss, honestly, I was just putting it in my bag for later and that's the truth". She went red in the face and said "Did I ask you for your comments? No, I did not and I can assure you, Lara, that you wouldn't know the truth if it hit you in the face". I said "I don't think you're being fair" and I wasn't loud - I know I wasn't. I kept thinking of my script - keep it quiet, keep it quiet - over and over again in my head. But then she said "Right - that's it - get out - go to Mr Thomas and tell him you're on detention for bringing food into the classroom and then lying about it".
Teacher:	And did you go?
Lara:	Of course.
Teacher:	Quietly - like we agreed?

Lara:	No...I kicked my table over and called her a name, so I suppose I really blew it. That's why I got a double detention, five minus points and the letter home.
Teacher:	Pretty bad eh? It was a shame about the name calling though.
Lara:	Yeah but she asked for it...
Teacher:	Hold on. Remember it's not her we're talking about here - it's you. You agreed your targets and you did meet two of them - the lining up and getting in quietly, and for the first bit, keeping your voice quiet and not shouting out. We know what the three warnings system is and it didn't happen today. That's a fact and we can't change it. Nonetheless, you still need to do the 'right' thing and show the behaviours that will keep you in class.
Lara:	What - like just shut up?
Teacher:	What do you think would have happened if you had?
Lara:	Well - I suppose if I'd just played dumb and looked a bit sorry she might have got off my back - then I wouldn't be in a double detention.
Teacher :	Okay - so now you do the double detention because that's the system, but next time you can stop and think earlier, okay?
Lara:	Okay!

Teaching the concept

Knowing the rule

It will be useful to have the school rules and discipline procedures photocopied onto cards. These can be used as a focus for conversations on the theme of 'What if you broke that rule? What would happen? What behaviours do you need to show in order to keep the rules?'

Acting it out/ roleplay

The students can create roleplays (based on both real and imaginary events) in which students break the rules or fall foul of the discipline policy for a variety of reasons. They can act out the more positive responses that will get them a better outcome, alongside those that will get them further trouble and sanctions. Once again, the scenes can be video-ed to allow for further reflection, discussion and analysis. The central focus here will be on knowing, using and transferring the kinds of positive behaviours demanded by the policy into the classroom.

Help us out

Students can work on a range of problem page letters (devised by them and the course facilitator) which detail incidents when students have broken the rules (on purpose and unintentionally). Students can work together to formulate the 'best' response/piece of advice to enable each character to work effectively within their own school's discipline framework.

Devise your own policy

Creating a policy from scratch is an interesting and often informative activity. The students can work together to define their own set of school rules and system of rewards and sanctions. They can choose at which point in the system the student should receive a detention (if they wish to incorporate this strategy) and at which point students should be told off, asked to leave the room, excluded for a day, rewarded for 'good' behaviour etc. Defining acceptable and unacceptable behaviour or 'good' and 'bad' behaviours will clearly be key to this process.

P.S.

- Sometimes it is useful to have a flow diagram of the school discipline policy. The students can place themselves within the structure and they are then able to visualise themselves moving up, down and within the system

- Often the student's anecdotal descriptions of the application of the school discipline structure can expose real problems with the whole school behaviour management system. A constructive way forward would be to find a channel to inform senior management of some of the difficulties. If appropriate, the students within the group may be involved in this process. They then end up as part of the mainstream culture by being part of the process that constructs the systems which run the culture

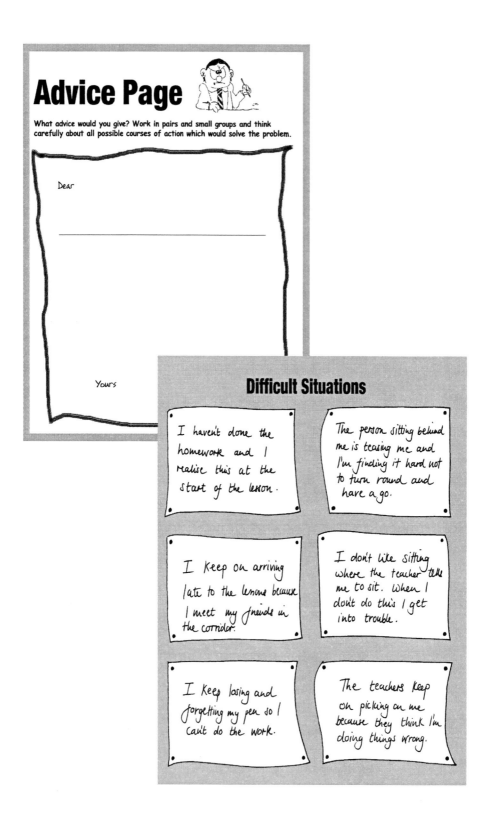

Advice Page

What advice would you give? Work in pairs and small groups and think carefully about all possible courses of action which would solve the problem.

Dear

_____

Yours

Difficult Situations

I haven't done the homework and I realise this at the start of the lesson.

The person sitting behind me is teasing me and I'm finding it hard not to turn round and have a go.

I keep on arriving late to the lessons because I meet my friends in the corridor.

I don't like sitting where the teacher tells me to sit. When I don't do this I get into trouble.

I keep losing and forgetting my pen so I can't do the work.

The teachers keep on picking on me because they think I'm doing things wrong.

CONCEPT 10
Working With a Model

Key concept

Behaviour is extremely complex, and it is a difficult task for students to be aware of and understand all the various inputs they experience, and the reasons why they behave as they do. The eternal question that will be asked of them is "but why did you do that? Why? Why? Why?" Their inability to answer this question may well be mistaken for impudence or a sign of disaffection when, in reality, they probably won't have a clue why they did it. In order to address this problem and begin to gain some clarity here, we propose the use of various models – not simply 'off the peg' versions, but those designed and constructed with and by the students themselves, and helping them to understand and perceive their own behaviours.

One such model, designed and constructed by a female student, consisted of her visualising her adrenal glands, which she could point to at the top of her kidneys, as having a hot line route to her jaw muscles. When stimulated through stress or anger her adrenal glands release a chemical into her blood – Adrenaline – which would go straight to her jaw muscles, causing her to become, in her words, a "loud mouth that couldn't shut up." Clearly, this model was very individual in the sense that it was personal to her and designed and constructed by her and the facilitator. These kinds of 'personal' models are very powerful and effective in that they are 'owned' by the student, but there are also many 'off the peg' models which can be adopted for individual use – anger management models, stress bucket models, and so on.

Illustrative script
Brainy behaviour

Teacher: Okay. Today's session is called 'Brainy Behaviour' - any ideas as to what I might be talking about?

Cara: How we can show we're brainy by doing the 'right' behaviours?

Tom: Yeah, like you have to be a dunce or something or maybe brain dead to do the wrong thing in class?

Teacher: Umm...sort of. It is about the brain and about how you can change certain behaviours - by learning and practising new ones. What we're going to focus on is how the brain controls all actions, and the fact that some thoughts are automatic but they can also be changed. Okay - have a look at these cards and see if you can tell me which behaviours you think that the brain has total control over...

Tom: I think 'breathing' because you'd die otherwise.

Cara: And your heart rate, as it needs to keep going and going.

Teacher: Okay - what about these other behaviours - reading, writing and moving your arms and legs? Does the brain have total control there? Do you have total control?

Cara: No...because you can choose to read or write and move about.

Teacher: Great! So they are actions that you have voluntary control over. You can control them yourself through practice.

Cara: And if you practice then you'll get better at them - like us with using our scripts - we actually can get better at doing the right behaviour in class.

Teacher: Is it actually that easy though - at first?

Tom: No - because it's like you've got into a habit and you almost seem to do it without thinking. You need to start at the beginning again - almost like you're learning something new that you didn't know before.

Teacher: So you've got to back and perhaps actually think about how you do learn 'new' things or behaviours. For example, if you were learning to skateboard or roller skate for the first time - how would you do it? What would be the first stage?

Cara:	Well, the first bit is when you go round really slowly because you can't quite get your balance. You hold onto anyone or anything that you can find so that you don't fall over and hurt yourself.
Tom:	Yeah - and when you do fall everyone takes the mick.
Teacher:	And does that make you want to give up?
Tom:	Nah! - I'd be more determined than ever to show them.
Teacher:	Okay - so what's the next stage?
Tom:	Well - I suppose it's when you feel more confident and you can move around on your own without holding onto anything.
Teacher:	And then?
Cara:	You can probably whizz around really fast without even thinking about it - like it's become automatic to you.
Teacher:	Okay - let's relate this back to our behaviour then. There must be loads of behaviours that are automatic that we've seen each other do in class. Any ideas?
Tom:	Talking - I just do it automatically - as soon as I go in and sit down I've got to talk to my mates.
Cara:	Or shouting out - he does that and I fidget about a lot - I can't help it, I just fiddle with stuff on my desk and it drives the teachers mad.
Teacher:	Okay - so it's like you've learnt these behaviours and they've become automatic - like a washing machine - you just switch it on and there it goes.
Cara:	Yeah - but you can stop a washing machine - you can switch it off again.
Teacher:	Right - and what I'm trying to get across to you today is that you can also change these automatic behaviours. You can intercept them with new behaviours and these can then become automatic instead.
Cara:	Ah - so it really is what I'm doing when I use my script in my head - every time that the teacher accuses me of not listening when I really was - I just say 'ignore the bore' again and again in my head while I look straight at him and make out that I'm listening for England.
Tom:	Yeah - so you don't get gobby back - that's becoming the automatic behaviour.

Cara:	But it has taken weeks - I couldn't do it before last week - I needed to keep on and on practising it - it's not easy to tell your brain to tell your body to do something new.
Teacher:	But you've proved you can do it, and consequently met your target every day since Monday - and you've done the same Tom. Now you can both work on new ones - like the chatting and fiddling. What you have to remember at all times is that once you become aware that you are following the brain's commands - you can stop them. There are lots of strategies to use - like stopping and thinking about the way you really want to behave and using the self-talk scripts. Most important - you need to really believe in yourself that you can do it. Okay?
Tom & Cara:	Okay.

Part of the power of such models lies in the 'code' that they provide students – one which allows them to talk about behaviour in such a way that is meaningful and personal to them. For example, the visual imagery of certain models provides a very immediate means of identifying and describing both feelings and behaviours. How full is your stress bucket? How far up the thermometer is your anger? Allowing and encouraging students to actually build their own models also makes use of this kind of visualisation – what would my anger look like if it was a shape/ a colour? The idea is to provide the behaviour with a structure or form, which then allows you to talk about behaviour with a shared and secure understanding. Also, there is an element of de-personalisation that is helpful here, as the students can talk about their behaviour in a way that is not directly personal. As with role-play techniques, this creates a 'safe' environment in which to discuss behaviour in a non-threatening and non-judgmental way.

Illustrative script
Traffic lights

Teacher:	Okay Jan - we've been working on your model for the last couple of weeks and you've been able to make good use of it in order to cope with your anger in a range of situations. Can you talk us through your model?

Jan: Yeah, mine's the traffic lights. I wanted to use them because it was something that I could picture in my own head and I thought it would help me to stop before I opened my mouth and got myself into bigger trouble. When I felt that surge of hot, red anger boiling up, I would think 'red' and picture the traffic lights in my head and say, 'stop' to myself - like this [shows the traffic light poster to the group]. When I said, 'stop' it was to stop and think about what I was about to do - so, not just reacting, but being proactive and stopping myself from acting in an aggressive way. So the first thing is to stop and calm myself down - just by using that script and clenching my fists - like I'm holding the anger down and pushing it down to the floor. I'd then be saying: "What's going on here? What is the problem and how do I feel about it?" I'd then be thinking ahead and picturing the amber light.

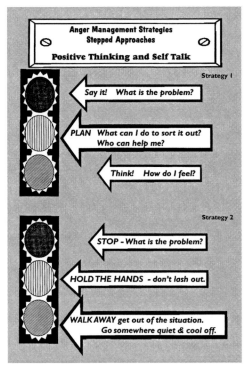

The amber light is the longest part really because I'd then be thinking about consequences and working out what would happen if? That's the next bit of the script in my model: What would happen if I did this/ that? Would it get me the best possible outcome? So, I'd list them like a shopping list in my head. If the teacher had refused to explain something to me again because she said I wasn't listening when I had been, I would think and feel very angry like I wanted to shout at her - I'd stop with the red light and then wait and plan with the amber light:

- So, what if I shouted back - then I'd get chucked out
- What if I said nothing and asked my friend n I'd be in class but still might get told off if she saw me chatting again

- What if I zipped up and said nothing - just had a
  go. Then I'd not be in trouble and if I really couldn't
  get it, then I could go and ask her at the end of
  the lesson.

I'd choose to go with the last one - even though it would
be the hardest - because I'd be feeling angry and a bit fed
up that I couldn't really understand it, but I'd have to
hold those feelings for the next 45 minutes or so. That
would be the green light as I'd be going with my best
plan then. I think this model has helped me to stop
being so impulsive and to think before I act instead of
just jumping in. It's hard work though.

Teacher: Yeah - I'd agree that it's hard work, but you really know
how to use this model now, so no doubt it will get easier
as time goes on.

Jan: Practice makes perfect Miss!

Teaching the concept

Designing your model
Students can design and make up their own models (2D/3D) and then
be encouraged to explain these to the rest of the group. What will be
most important is to ensure that it actually works in practice, so we
would recommend that use of the model be directly linked to the
student's weekly target(s). For example, one of Jan's targets may read: I
will use the traffic light method every time I feel angry so that I can
stop and prevent myself from lashing out. Students may wish to
formulate presentations and have session time allocated for this
purpose each week or to have one whole session to focus on building
their models.

Teaching a range of models
Anger management: There are a wide range of models for teaching
and practising anger management strategies and techniques. It is
clearly useful for students to have access to these during the *School
Survival* course. These may include the following:

Traffic lights (as introduced before). This model provides a stepped
approach to solving problems, including those that cause students to
become angry and confrontational. Visualising the STOP, WAIT and

GO lights, and making use of solution-focused approaches to solve problems can be adopted and rehearsed on a regular basis in order to achieve a better outcome for the student. The process might be visualised using the traffic light chart (page 125)

Scaling 1-10. Students can visualise a scale from 1-10 and work out where they are on the scale at the time they are experiencing high levels of anger or anxiety. They can then take a deep breath and visualise themselves moving down the scale, identifying what they should do in order to reach the lower end of the scale and gain control.

Post-it notes. Students can write down specific problems onto post-it notes, accurately describing both their feelings and the causes of those feelings. This model enables the student to 'return' to the problem at a later stage, and is most useful when they are in a situation that can't be sorted out straight away. The action of 'posting it' is symbolic and allows the individual to calm down, knowing that they can pick the problem up at a later stage and then begin to work on more positive responses and solutions.

'Bin it'! As with post-it notes, this is a tool for students to use when they know they cannot deal with the situation effectively at the time that it occurs. Students can visualise the problem or their anger being thrown into a rubbish bin and the lid being held down to contain it. This can be taken off at a later stage when they feel calmer and more rational.

Cool off time. At times, it may be necessary to take time-out to 'cool off'. This is a preventative approach and would need to be agreed in advance with staff. The trick here is to enable a student to accurately spot the precursors to an explosive outburst.

Coping with stress
Much like anger management models, these models help students understand feelings and emotions that may well appear overwhelming.

Stress bucket. Often, giving a student a visual model of how stress can accumulate over time and then can lead to an outburst or inability to deal with a minor difficulty is useful. In this model, everybody has a stress bucket located inside them. Things that cause stress gradually fill up the bucket, until it overflows and we can't take any more stress – hence the angry outburst. Students use the model to look at what is causing stress, how to stop the stress filling their bucket, how to empty the bucket of stress, and how to spot when the bucket is nearly full and about to overflow.

Thermometer. This works in much the same way as the traffic light, but is a visual model which helps pupils describe how stressed they may be feeling. Using a scale of 1-100 degrees centigrade is often an accessible way for students to describe their temperature and level of stress.

Using scientific models
When the students explore the physiology of their anger or reaction to stress, and the biology behind their emotions, the models that science presents to help the students understand these complicated processes are often useful in helping students understand what is going on inside them at times of difficulty.

Adrenaline - flight or fight response. Explaining the power of adrenaline is often a useful way of getting a student to understand what is happening to their bodies at times of stress or anxiety. Using the caveman and the bear as an example of fighting or running is useful as it attempts to show how this hormone can be positive. Getting the students to visualise this chemical going through their blood vessels and affecting the organs it reaches, helps apply the effects of adrenaline to their own personal feelings and experiences.

P.S.

- Collect model making materials to enable the student to make models of their anger. Using other forms of art will often let them express their feelings and emotions where words may fail.

- Different forms of music can be used to represent different moods and can be used by some students who are into music culture to 'mix' up a musical model of the way that they work.

Some Further Thoughts

Delivering the impossible – the role of the facilitator

It is essential that the facilitator is the 'right' person and has the 'right' skills to be able to deliver a *School Survival* course. This is an enormous task and demands the kind of qualities and skills that are evident in those who really deliver 'best practice' in the classroom on a consistent (daily) basis and have the experience of including those pupils at risk of exclusion. What is also usually of some importance is the actual position that is held by the facilitator within the school. The students do perceive and understand the hierarchies that exist within schools and often afford greater acknowledgement (and sometimes fear and respect) to those nearer the top end of the hierarchy. If the facilitator is seen and perceived by other students (and other members of staff), as someone who is important and central to the school as an institution, then this will ensure that the group's profile and status is immediately raised. The intervention will have an entirely different status for those students targeted. However, we might wish that staff are seen as being on an equal footing. In the eyes of the students this is clearly not the case, and we do need to profit from this perception – whether or not we feel that such views are politically or ethically correct. Opting for a senior member of staff to facilitate the group sends a very clear message to the students involved, and to the rest of the school as a whole. However, a higher position also brings with it difficulties, as does simply identifying those who have good classroom practice. Being a deputy head in charge of discipline, who can control even the most disruptive class in the school, does not necessarily mean they are the person who is best able to lead a supportive group that will illicit genuine change in the target pupils. There is no right and wrong here, but it is very important to be aware of the status and skills of whoever is to run the group. Consequently, it is very important to ensure a balanced approach in terms of allocating this role to a member of staff in any school. It is clearly the personal qualities and skills of that individual which will be the most important consideration here. These will probably include the following:

- Understanding group processes
- Being able to reflect
- Being able to listen
- The ability to stay calm under pressure
- Good organisational skills
- Being able to see things in the moment
- Having a good understanding of how behaviour can be learnt and changed
- Empathy and security for feelings and situations of others
- Self-awareness of own values, beliefs, attitudes and principles
- A level of personal self-esteem and confidence which can, in turn, facilitate the growth of others in these areas, empowering them to help themselves
- Being able to adopt a flexible approach
- Not needing to feel 'in control' all the time
- Having good skills in terms of giving feedback to the students
- Being able to effectively co-ordinate and liaise with staff
- Being able to cope effectively with personal stressors
- Being able to manage the stress experienced and projected by students and other members of staff
- Having an adequate personal support network to ensure and maintain emotional and physical well-being
- Excellent communication skills in all areas
- Adequate time and resources (this doesn't equate to thousands of Pounds, but crucially, adequate time and resources to carry out the intervention properly. Time will need to be created in the timetable and a commitment given that the facilitator will not cover for absent colleagues. Time will also be needed for adequate co-ordination and effective planning)

The role of the facilitator is a tricky one. However, it is important to stress that we do not propose a 'right' or 'perfect' way of doing this job. There is no such thing as the perfect facilitator who adopts the right way. There is no 'right' way – only those which are better than others. A key element is always that of trial and error, that clearly pre-supposes the ability to reflect upon practice – perhaps the most important and crucial skill of any group facilitator.

Making sure that the progress continues

As stated previously, we feel that any intervention of this kind should be time-constrained, and the processes that the students go through should culminate at an end point that also identifies the way forward in terms of maintaining the progress made. Clearly, the level and amount of input and support that individual students will require will be dependent not only upon the progress made, but also their personal starting points. On any continuum – including an EBD one – there will be students who are at the top end and will usually require a greater level of support and on-going input in order to ensure that progress can and does continue. It may well be possible, at the end of the course, to identify each student as falling into one of three categories:

Firstly, there will be those students who have benefited from the course. They will have learnt 'enough', changed their behaviour 'enough' and experienced a level of positive feedback that will, in turn, ensure a level of confidence and self-esteem that allows future success to remain well within their grasp. The changes will have been made concrete and cemented in place, and will subsequently remain with and within the student once this regular and on-going level of support has been withdrawn. Just as with a well-built wall – it will remain standing and will require minimal maintenance, but will need a little painting and cleaning occasionally. Such students can be encouraged and monitored by the existing school systems and the facilitator may well contribute to these, but without having to have any further, ongoing, direct input.

Secondly, there will be a group of students who may well make up a significant portion of the targeted group as a whole, and these students will be those who will continue to need some support in the future. It is important to highlight the fact that once the group process has ended, and the students are no longer working together with the facilitator on a regular basis, then the role of the facilitator in relation to the students will inevitably change. While the group work was ongoing, the facilitator would be aware of and involved in the student's experiences on an almost daily basis. This role would diminish once the group sessions are stopped, and the facilitator's relationship would be very much based upon history. If that history is not relevant to what's going on in the here and now, then the effectiveness of the work or input by the facilitator will decay. What does then need to be recognised is that if the group sessions or work are to cease, the facilitator will be entering a new phase in terms of supporting the students involved. This will be a phase of one to one support that will not allow for the same kind of reliance upon the benefits that previously resulted from the group work.

This one to one ongoing support will need to build on the completed work and the skills learnt, and provide an appropriate level of mentoring, based upon the needs and requirements of each individual student. It may be possible, and sometimes preferable, for the facilitator to take on this role, or it may be necessary and advisable to allocate this work to another member of staff with whom the student is most likely to be able to form and sustain a productive and positive relationship. If the latter option is chosen, it will obviously be necessary for this member of staff to be introduced to the student and spend some quality time with him/ her prior to the end of the group sessions. This transfer time does need to be timetabled in order to ensure that the student does not experience an abrupt change and the sense of loss and insecurity that so often results from badly planned 'quick fixes'. The 'weaning' process away from the group stage to the individual support stage needs to be both gently and carefully structured. There will need to be some form of contract or agreement about what this support actually means and entails – does it mean meeting twice a week or once a week? In a lunch break or after school?

What is important here is how the course facilitator also engages and liaises with those in the school who are going to take on this mentoring role (whether these are members of SMT, form tutors or learning support assistants). Clearly, there should have been ongoing liaison and consultation with staff throughout the intervention, and this will have allowed staff to fully appreciate and understand both the ethos and content of the group. In addition, the way in which the students will have been supported, listened to, helped to change and modify their behaviours, and all the skills and concepts learnt, and covered will need to be incorporated and further built upon in this one to one context. It is crucial that there is a shift in focus – transferring the support networks for these students from the facilitator onto the rest of the school staff. A measure of the success of the facilitator and the intervention as a whole is the extent to which this is achieved and maintained. This practice and philosophy needs to become central to the school systems and must be adopted by staff, as a whole, if students are to truly build upon the progress made and remain included within the school context. It is not just the job of the facilitator to ensure this inclusion, but rather the duty of the school as a whole to ensure that every student's needs are met, both currently and in the future.

Once the mentors have been identified, it may be useful for the facilitator to offer some sessions in order to highlight and reinforce the work covered in the group. A powerful and useful means of transferring this information is to ask the students to present their views about what they have done and learnt, and how they may have been able to effect certain changes. Devising and delivering a presentation of this kind, in which they could present such concepts as locus of control, physiology, their models for behaviour and so on, would also formalise the handing over process and even allow for a 'graduation' session, in which the students graduate from the group to the individualised programme of support.

Within this 'mid range' or second category, there will be students who require very different levels of support, and this will need to be defined and allocated prior to the end of the group intervention. Subsequent to this, it will be necessary to have some form of monitoring system in place for all students (regardless of the level of one to one mentoring input), in order to identify exactly how they're getting on and coping in school. This should then provide the necessary information to make any future decisions about whether this 'new' support is, and continues to be, adequate, or if a new or alternative approach needs to be adopted. If this is not provided, then the situation can quickly go downhill.

Such a negative scenario may well be most associated with the third category of students – those whose original difficulties were pronounced and significant and who may find the task of changing their behaviours too substantial. These are the students who will demand and need more support. This may well involve the facilitator setting up and delivering a follow-up course. It is also important to recognise that there are likely to be a minority of students who will need a high level of support and intervention throughout the rest of their school careers, if they are to survive and succeed in school. This fact does not mean that the facilitator and the intervention have failed. It never was a 'turn around and mend them' course, and didn't set out to present itself as such. This intervention was about moving the situation to a better position for each student, and should consequently be deemed to be a success, even if the movement in the 'right' direction was very small.

However, the 'better position' achieved or arrived at by some students will still not be enough in terms of enabling them to survive independently in school. It is at this point that the facilitator will need to carefully analyse what it is that enables the student to 'hold on' and 'survive' when supported in the group. Is it the one to one attention of the facilitator? Is it the support? Is it the process of behavioural change? If it is about these factors, then it will be essential to arrange for these things to be available to the student on an ongoing basis. A combination of one to one mentoring and group work will need to be devised and delivered, alongside a system of careful and supportive monitoring which ensures close liaison and links with parents or carers.

When the interventions and support systems are not enabling the student to move forward and effect and maintain real change, it is vital to pose the question: is the support offered really what the student needs? In most cases, in our experience, this kind of ongoing support is usually appropriate. However, in a few rare cases, it is not. These are the 'long-termers' who require extremely careful consideration. It may be that a further group and one to one intervention programme which is more finely tuned to their individual needs may have some impact. It may be that more intensive one to one support or small group work (three pupils maximum), in which the focus is upon revisiting what has been covered in the initial group intervention, will be beneficial. In this group there can be an emphasis on encouraging peers to support each other in coping with the situations and events they encounter on an almost daily basis. This is almost a case of continually repairing and looking after the foundations of the wall. Where subsidence has occurred, the damage is deeper and greater and the job of repairing takes longer. The foundations have to be dug almost twice as deep as previously, before the damage can even begin to be repaired. However, we would argue that this task is worthwhile, and that it is the duty and responsibility of schools to ensure that even those with the most damaged foundations are given the chance to dig deep and rebuild their lives. They have the right to this opportunity and we have the duty to ensure that they have every chance to survive and succeed within the school context. We may knock down the wall if it has been badly built, but we don't build it up again until the foundations are right.

Additional Stuff – Teaching the Concepts

The following chapter is an example of a programme that has been carried out with students. It covers many of the areas discussed in the book and gives a structure to the intervention. It is presented here in the way in which it was presented to the students.

- **Locus of Control**: Where does control for event lie? Within the person or externally?
- **How the Brain Works**: Looking at the physiology of the brain; the centres for emotion; my reptilian brain; where I do my thinking; the cortex; reflexes; and the lack of control
- **Anger Management Skills**: How can I develop a model for my anger so that I am then able to develop strategies to control it?
- **Assertiveness Skills**: How can I get what I want without being aggressive or angry? What does passive mean?
- **Problem Solving Strategies**: There are lots of different ways of solving problems, but it is possible to have a framework to help solve all problems. A brief guide to solution-focused therapy
- **Body Language**: If you can read a person's body language, then you can read their mind. If you can do this, it is much easier to stay out of trouble. How can you change the messages that your body is giving out to get you a better outcome?
- **Social Skills**: What are social skills? What social skills do I already have and how can I build on those that are not as good? What stops me from getting on with other students?
- **Emotional Intelligence**: Did you know that there are different ways of being intelligent? Let's look at you and see what things you are good at!
- **Conflict Resolution**: Sometimes we get into conflict and arguments. What are the best ways to avoid them and what can we do to sort things out when we are in the middle of the confrontation, and afterwards?
- **Simple Physiology**: What is it inside my body that makes me feel the way I do? Let's look at the science

- **How to Describe Behaviour**: We need to be able to observe and describe behaviour accurately and fairly. We need to be able to see how one thing leads to another. This is going to need careful observation and analysis. Let's watch some behaviour and see what we can learn from what we see
- **Setting Targets**: We need to set targets to see how well we are doing and where we are going
- **Having a Good Argument**: Arguments don't always mean you have to hate someone. It is possible to disagree with someone and still like them. What makes a good argument and what makes a bad argument?
- **How to Say Sorry Like You Mean it**: Sometimes you might be sorry for something that you have done. Now you need to make sure that you show the outside world that you are sorry. It might even be a good idea to show that you're sorry, when perhaps you don't feel that strongly about it
- **Future Basing/My Excellent Future**: Where do I want to be in the future? What will it look, feel and smell like? What is the first step to getting there? Did you know that sports people use this technique to develop their skills?
- **Empathy**: Do I understand how other people tick? How they feel? Can I understand how my enemy feels? What's it like to be someone else?
- **Secret Signs**: How can I support my friends in a lesson by giving them a sign to remind them about all the things that we have done in the sessions
- **Stress Management Skills**: Everybody gets stressed. So how do you manage it?

References

de Shazar, S. (1988) *Clues: Investigating Solutions in Brief Therapy*, New York, Norton

Elias, M.J., Clabby J., (1992) *Building Social and Emotional Development in Deaf Children.* The PATH programme, Seattle, University of California Press

Faupel, A., Herrick, E. & Sharp, P. (1998) *Anger Management – A Practical Guide*, London, David Fulton Publishers

Furman, B. & Ahola, T. (1992) *Solution Talk: Hosting Therapeutic Conversations.* New York, Norton

Goleman, D. (1995) *Emotional Intelligence – Why it can matter more than IQ,* London, Bloomsbury

Gourley, P. (1999) *Teaching Self Control in the Classroom – a Cognitive Behavioural Approach*, Bristol, Lucky Duck Publishing

Greenberg, M.T. & Kusche, C.A. (1993) *Promoting Social and Emotional Development in Deaf Children.* The PATH programme, Seattle, University of California Press

Johnson, P. & Rae, T. (1999) *Crucial Skills – An Anger Management and Problem Solving Teaching Programme for High School Students*, Bristol, Lucky Duck Publishing

Rae, T. (1998) *Dealing with Feeling,* Bristol, Lucky Duck Publishing

Rae, T. (2000) *Confidence, Assertiveness, Self-Esteem – A Series of 12 Sessions for Secondary School Students*, Bristol, Lucky Duck Publishing

Rae, T. (2001) *Strictly Stress – Effective Stress Management for High School Students*, Bristol, Lucky Duck Publishing

Rhodes, J. & Ajmal, Y. (1995) *Solution Focused Thinking in Schools*, London, Brief Therapy Publication

Sheldon, B. (1995) *Cognitive Behavioural Therapy: Research, Practice and Philosophy*, London, Routledge

Warden, D. & Christie, D. (1997) *Teaching Social Behaviour*, London, David Fulton Publishers

White, M. (1999) *Picture This, Guided Imagery for Circle Time*, Bristol, Lucky Duck Publishing